AF409271

Husband Killer Donna Yaklich

Jessi Dixon

Published by Trellis Publishing, 2021.

While every precaution has been taken in the preparation of this book, the publisher assumes no responsibility for errors or omissions, or for damages resulting from the use of the information contained herein.

HUSBAND KILLER DONNA YAKLICH

First edition. June 29, 2021.

Copyright © 2021 Jessi Dixon.

ISBN: 979-8224682331

Written by Jessi Dixon.

HUSBAND KILLER

DONNA YAKLICH

JESSI DIXON

DONNA YAKLICH

Old-fashioned police work

In December 1985, a narcotics detective was shot and killed in the driveway of his farm in Pueblo, Colorado, where he lived with his five children and his wife, Donna Yaklich. Initially, authorities suspected Dennis' death was linked to his work in law enforcement, but a tip led them to two teenage shooters – and eventually, back to Dennis' wife, Donna.

However, attorneys for Donna Yaklich argued that Dennis had been beating his wife. The murder, they claimed, was a battered woman's desperate attempt to escape a lifetime of abuse – or potentially becoming a murder victim herself, like Dennis' first wife, who is thought to have died of a diet drug overdose in 1977.

Yaklich was finally acquitted of first-degree murder after a mistrial and a second trial that has been described as "grueling," but was convicted on the charge of conspiracy for hiring gunmen to kill her husband. Her sentence was forty years in prison, but was released to a halfway house in 2005, after serving close to eighteen years.

The young men Yaklich had hired to carry out the murder were also arrested and sentenced. Charles Greenwell, who was only 16 when the crime was committed, received a sentence of twenty years while his brother Eddie, who had been 25, received thirty years.

However, while Yaklich's claims of abuse weren't enough to get her off on the premise of self-defence, they did encourage authorities to reopen their investigation into the death of Barbara Yaklich. According to a cold case team, the investigation was "incomplete."

"This case needed some good, old-fashioned police work," said team lead Steve Johnson, with the Colorado Bureau of Investigation. "In my opinion, I have seen better documented traffic accidents."

Discrepancies were found in the autopsy report, which originally claimed Barbara had fainted from taking diet pills. When her body-builder husband, Dennis, tried "energetically" to resuscitate her, she suffered bleeding in her abdomen. However, administering CPR is not an appropriate reaction to fainting – and as a police officer trained in CPR, Dennis would have known this.

Still, there was apparently no examination of the potential crime scene, and when Dennis was asked to take a polygraph to support his defense, he refused.

Denver-area pathologist Michael Doberson determined that the conclusions in the report were "very unusual" – the internal damage Barbara had suffered, he claimed, was more likely caused by a blow to the abdomen. Doberson included his findings in a letter to Johnson dated in 2005, stating that in his opinion, "the entire scenario is simply not credible." A second forensic pathologist concurred with Doberson's conclusions.

According to reports, Barbara's liver tore open and her abdomen was quickly filled with more than 2,000 millilitres of blood – nearly 40 per cent of her total blood volume, and more than twice as much as is typical in a victim of a fatal car accident.

Investigators are now considering her death as "suspicious," with the tear caused by a blunt force trauma consistent with "punches and knee drops to the upper abdomen," according to pathologist Stephen Cina. However, the autopsy report showed no other indications that would reveal a pattern of abuse – no recorded discoloration, bruising, or external signs of beatings.

While the investigation into Barbara's death is now complete, the case hasn't been closed. According to the coroner and the Pueblo County Sheriff, the public deserves answers to the questions that have been raised.

The family man

Donna Yaklich met Dennis and his children only a few months after Barbara's death. According to Yaklich, the plan was to move in with the family for the summer and help him get the kids back into their home, since they were temporarily staying with Dennis' mother.

"I had no expected to fall in love with the children, who so desperately needed someone," Yaklich said. "They were grieving for their mother, so I couldn't bear to leave them."

Barbara had died on Valentine's Day, and had "appeared fine" as her children left for school that morning. However, an hour later, Barbara was dead – and Dennis was the only person who had been with her as she died. According to some reports, there are members of the community who do continue to question Dennis' involvement in the death of his first wife, including at least one of his former co-workers.

"Dennis' fellow officers knew he was out of control, but they also knew when they needed him he would be the first to go through the door," Yaklich said. "No one who worked with him would go against him."

It was this feeling of hopelessness that eventually led Yaklich to hire gunmen to kill her husband, in an effort to finally end the ongoing abuse. She'd moved in with Dennis when she was only 22 and he was 30. The children were aged 3, 9, 11, and 12 – and she immediately fell into the role of step-mother, despite the abuse which began only a month after Yaklich moved in. She said she attempted to leave a few times, but always went back.

"I feared Dennis, but at the same time I felt at home with him because I had grown up in an abusive environment," Yaklich said. "I fell into the trap of thinking if I could make everything perfect for him, he wouldn't get mad at me or at the kids. Dennis' threats to kill me or kill someone I loved if I ever left again kept me there."

Dennis even threatened to use his access to federal law enforcement agents against Yaklich, telling her that she'd never be able to get away from him – these agents were capable of fiding anyone, anywhere. Eventually, she said, "I lost myself. I lost hope."

"I became very depressed and mad at myself because I had no trusted my instincts about leaving the relationship when the abuse started," Yaklich said. "Suicidal thoughts became an answer. Then came homicidal thoughts."

Looking back, Yaklich admitted that she wished she had listened to those first instincts, but eventually came to a point where she no longer cared. However, she said she has been working on bettering herself since being convicted and sentenced.

"Being in prison is similar to the prison I put myself in while I was married to Dennis," she said. "However, prison is also what you make of it, so I've enrolled in educational programs, had therapy, and also taken care of myself. Things I should have done in society."

A professional abuser

At a menacing 6'5" and 280 pounds, Dennis Yaklich was a competitive weightlifter who continuously used steroids to supplement his workouts – despite the fact that they also enhanced his aggressive tendencies. While the officers who worked with him conceded that he was always the go-to guy for breaking down a door or clearing a room, he was difficult to manage. In fact, when he did become confrontational, even a supervisor threatened to shoot him because they had no other way to defend themselves.

A former partner once stated that he felt he always had to "clean up after Dennis," and other co-workers have admitted they "dreaded" working with Dennis, because of his aggressive and unpredictable behaviour. Some of his closest colleagues have even confessed that Dennis displayed some "abusive tactics" on the job – while denying the complaints of citizens against him.

Yaklich endured what can only be described as domestic terrorism. While the physical abuse, which included slapping, choking, kicking, and pushing her down stairs as well as sadistic sexual assaults, was indeed disabling and troubling, the psychological abuse was almost worse. According to Yaklich, the threat of death loomed constantly – Dennis would put his gun to her head and threaten to kill her, point his finger at her in the shape of a gun and blow on it after miming shooting her with it, and even beating her under the cover of darkness so she wouldn't be able to prepare for the blows.

The physical abuse has been corroborated by a number of independent witnesses, including a mailman who reported seeing bruises on Yaklich's face, and a telephone repairman who had been called in twice to fix phones after Dennis had yanked them out of the wall in a fit of rage.

Following Yaklich's arrest, the repairman spoke with detectives investigating Dennis' death and said the bruises he had seen on Yaklich's neck and cheek were so prominent, he noticed them "at a glance." The detective inquired how the repairman could recall the incident so vividly, and he admitted that in his line of work, he sees "a lot of things like that in the low income areas and the projects, but I was shocked to see a cop's wife all bruised up like she was."

Cries unheard

Yaklich's first documented attempt for police intervention came in 1982, when she called Dennis' partner to explain that Dennis was "out of control" and threatening to kill her. The detective advised her to leave right away, but she said she was too afraid – if she left, she said, Dennis had told her he would kill her entire family, starting with her father.

Believing that Yaklich was in fear for her life, the detective immediately went to inform his supervisor about the call he'd received about his partner. According to the detective, the supervisor had gestured to indicate that he should just forget the call – it was none of their business – and the incident went unreported.

It was then that Yaklich realized that trying to get help from the police would be completely futile, and she would need to seek support elsewhere.

The next year, in November of 1983, Yaklich endured a short and traumatic visit with a psychologist. After Yaklich "sobbed uncontrollably" through the entire session, the psychologist recommended she leave her husband – but failed to offer her suggestions to muster the courage needed to do so, or what steps she could take to do it safely.

Since Yaklich was required to provide her abusive husband with detailed accounts of where she spent all her time, there was no way for her to continue therapy with regular appointments. She never went back for another session.

A few months later, Yaklich escaped to a battered women's shelter in Denver, in February of 1984. Dennis pleaded with her to come home, and even went so far as to promise that he would try to change – and because she was ashamed to go back to him again, Yaklich told the counselors that she was leaving the state.

Still, the abuse hadn't stopped another year later. Early in 1985, Yaklich tried talking to friends and family members – telling them she needed advice because Dennis was going to kill her. These claims were shrugged off by everyone she turned to, and the abuse began to escalate.

Feeling as though she had no other options, Yaklich began looking for an opportunity to kill herself. Her attempts failed, however, when she realized she would be abandoning her young son and step-children with their abusive father – and after witnessing the struggles of Barbara's children as they grieved the loss of their mother, she was unable to force that situation on her own child.

Later that year, the Pueblo Sheriff's Department received a 911 call from Yaklich's mother. One of the step-children had called Yaklich's parents after hearing what they thought was Dennis pushing Yaklich through a plate glass window. While it turned out that the noise was caused by just a bowl hitting the floor, the officers who responded barely acknowledged Yaklich.

In fact, their inspection of the situation involved a brief conversation with Dennis followed by a tour of the gym Dennis was building on the property. The situation only reinforced Yaklich's desperate situation on the other side of the blue line – living in fear of an abusive spouse with no support or protection from the authorities.

Finally, on December 12, 1985, one of Yaklich's friends finally responded to her pleas for help. A neighbour, Eddie Greenwell, waited at the Yaklich family's farm with his younger brother, Charles, into the early morning hours. When Dennis returned home after working a night shift, the brothers shot and killed him. Yaklich was inside the house, sleeping.

According to court documents, Yaklich had "approached several people" in an attempt to have her husband killed, and had met with Eddie Greenwell many times over a period of eight months. The Greenwell brothers were paid $4,200 in installments after the murder was committed – although the brothers testified they had been promised $45,000.

The story of the tragic marriage was detailed in a made-for-television movie called *Cries Unheard: The Donna Yaklich Story*. The film was released in 1994 and starred former Charlie's Angel Jaclyn Smith as Yaklich.

A disturbing conflict of interest

After Dennis was killed, the Pueblo Police Department – Dennis' employer – carried out an investigation into his death, despite the fact that the murder actually took place in the jurisdiction of the Pueblo Sheriff's Office. Lead roles in the inquiry were awarded to narcotics detectives – Dennis' partners.

The District Attorney was also a personal friend of Dennis', and even admitted to being a material witness in his own case. At the time of the trial, DA Sandstrom was wrapped up in a highly contested election – and this clear political agenda, combined with the attempts of the police department to hide its role in Yaklich's abuse and ultimately, Dennis' death, indicate incredible prejudice against Yaklich from the very beginning.

Not that Yaklich was surprised. After attempting to secure the help of police several times during the course of her abusive marriage, it was obvious to Yaklich that law enforcement was not on her side.

Still, the jury acquitted Yaklich of the charge of first-degree murder. Several jurors even thought Yaklich deserved to be acquitted of all charges, but felt intimidated by the Pueblo Police Department – and feared potential retaliation. Instead, the jury voted guilty on the charge of conspiracy to commit murder, believing that the fair-minded judge would give the battered wife the minimum sentence of eight years.

The probation supervisor who had conducted Yaklich's pre-sentencing investigation testified that Yaklich would be an "excellent candidate" for sentencing alternatives outside of the Department of Corrections, and gave the court his recommendation for the minimum sentence. His testimony affirmed the sense of desperation Yaklich claimed to be struggling with.

"I really felt that whether they did what she wanted done, to have Dennis killed, or whether Dennis found out and killed her, it didn't matter," he said. "She was at a point in her life where either was satisfactory."

However, the late Judge Seavy who presided over the trial chose to overlook the circumstances leading to Dennis' murder and remanded Yaklich to the Department of Corrections for a sentence of forty years. According to the judge, Yaklich "started this whole scenario," and therefore deserved to serve a period of time "in excess of the longest Greenwell's sentence."

"We cannot overlook the fact that Yaklich's participation in the death of her husband was not merely peripheral," stated court documents. "Had it not been for Yaklich, the Greenwells would not have been involved in this murder. Thus, in our view, we would be establishing poor public policy if Yaklich were to escape punishment by virtue of an unprecedented application of self-defense while the Greenwells were convicted of murder."

Still, the jurors were shocked and horrified by the severity of Judge Seavy's harsh sentence. More than half of the serving jurors submitted letters expressing their disappointment with the resulting sentence to a judge who presided over Yaklich's sentencing reconsideration a few years later. These letters were dismissed by that judge, however, who felt "that they must not allow for personal sympathy to influence their decision." Several of the jurors who served on the initial trial event went on to diligently advocate for Yaklich's early release, eighteen years later.

According to Dr. Lenore Walker, who counseled and evaluated Yaklich and provided expert testimony at her trial, Judge Seavy was "using the court and a woman's life to express his own ignorance of a battered woman's plight."

The conspiracy

According to court documents, Yaklich did receive payments totalling more than $250,000 under her late husband's three life insurance policies – leading to a theory that the motivation that pushed her to arrange her husband's death was to obtain this insurance money. The defense argued that Yaklich suffered from "battered woman syndrome," and that the conspiracy to commit murder was a "justifiable act of self-defence ... committed under duress resulting from years of physical and psychological battering by her husband."

"Yaklich lived in a constant state of fear of her husband," the defense argued. "At the time of his death, she believed she was in imminent danger of being killed by him or receiving great bodily injury from him."

The defense went on to explain that many battered women are unable to safely leave their abusive spouses – and in fact, the abuse often escalates as a result of a separation. Abusers have also been known to pursue their victims after they've left, subjecting them to "brutal attacks."

"Additionally, battered women may not psychologically or emotionally have the alternative of leaving the abuser because of their low self-esteem, their emotional and economic dependency, the absence of another place to go, and the woman's legitimate fear of the abuser's response to her leaving," stated the defense. "Battered women become trapped in their own fear and often feel that their only recourse is to kill the batterer or be killed."

Several people involved with the case, including District Attorney Sandstrom, have stated that if Yaklich had gone ahead and committed the murder herself, "she would have walked." However, the DA and many others also question the validity of Yaklich's testimony, including that Dennis was abusing her – maintaining the theory that Yaklich conspired to have him killed just to receive the insurance money.

The DA even stated that "if she had shot him herself, there would be no issue" – leading some to wonder if Sandstrom sees money as an acceptable motive for murder, as long as you follow through with it on your own.

Like most battered women, Yaklich both loved and hated her husband. Killing him herself would have been difficult, as she was afraid that as soon as she pointed a gun at him to save herself and her children, the love she had for him would "override her fear of him," and cause her to second-guess her decision. The ramifications from that could have bene deadly.

Another concern for Yaklich was her husband's established persona of invincibility – one he had carefully instilled in her over years of repeated psychological and physical abuse. Not only did Yaklich struggle to trust in her own ability to kill her husband, she struggled to believe that he would ever really die.

One of the prosecution's expert witnesses, Dr. Alice Brill, said in her testimony that Yaklich didn't meet the traditional profile of a battered woman. These women, according to Brill, generally kill their spouses with little premeditation and show little interest in pursuing relationships with other men – while Yaklich spent at least ten months planning her husband's murder, and had had at least one extramarital affair about a year before Dennis was killed.

Dennis' children also continue to question Yaklich's testimony, stating that none of them had ever witnessed any physical abuse from Dennis during the eight years of the couple's marriage. After Yaklich's parole hearing in October 2005, Dennis' daughter Vanessa fought back tears while talking about the court's decision to release Yaklich after she'd only served eighteen years of her forty-year sentence.

"It's devastating – I don't believe justice has prevailed," she said. "My father died at age 38. He was stripped of his opportunity to live life. He was prevented from raising his children, from seeing us grow up and accomplishing our goals."

Vanessa stated that Yaklich's claims of beatings and abuse were "an outright lie" – and that the depiction of the family's life shown in the TV-movie *Cries Unheard* were based entirely on prison interviews with Yaklich herself, with no supporting evidence or facts contributed by other relatives or friends.

Vanessa added that just two months before her father was killed, Yaklich had told her that Dennis had asked for a divorce – but that the couple planned to delay the proceedings until after the Christmas holidays, for the sake of the younger children. This story has been corroborated by Dennis' brother, who said Dennis told him over the phone that he planned to divorce Yaklich once the holidays had passed.

"(Dennis') life was taken because he was going to divorce my step-mother and not because she was the victim of abuse," Vanessa said. "I never feared my father, nor did I observe any abuse, whether it be psychological or physical, perpetrated by him. His demeanor was calm and loving, his words encouraging and supportive. I can honestly state my step-mother did not provide my siblings or myself with the same."

According to Vanessa, Yaklich didn't show any grief or remorse after Dennis had been killed – and even slapped Vanessa when she began to cry at her father's funeral. She went on to detail the ongoing "injustice," claiming to defend her father since he is no longer able to defend himself.

"My stepmother's legal defense was paid for by my father's life insurance proceeds and my family and I believe she profited from the made-for-television monstrosity," Vanessa said. "Most recently, her financial status has provided her with the ability to hire a media publicist."

Questions also remain about the relationship Yaklich had with her defense attorney, John Giduck. Records show Giduck and Yaklich took a romantic vacation to Jamaica together prior to her arrest in March 1986 – a getaway funded entirely from the death benefit Yaklich received after having her husband murdered.

In fact, the vacation was cut short when Yaklich was notified of the charges that were being brought against her, and surrendered to police upon her return to Pueblo. Most of the insurance money had already been spent by the time Yaklich was arrested.

According to information reported in the Colorado Springs Gazette, Yaklich had been involved in an extramarital affair about a year before Dennis' murder, and had begun a romantic relationship with Giduck only weeks after her husband's death. Giduck had apparently attended Dennis' funeral, where he had given Yaklich his business card and told him to call if she needed anything.

Yaklich reached out to him a few days later, after police asked her to verify the statement she'd given with a routine polygraph test.

A safe and abuse-free life

Still, Yaklich had a spotless record prior to her incarceration, which continued even after she was sent to prison – a testament to her strength of character. According to prison records, Yaklich managed to vigilantly avoid conflict and strictly followed the many rules surrounding prison life. Despite being forced into an environment filled with trouble, Yaklich managed to stay out of it through her entire eighteen-year term.

During her incarceration, Yaklich obtained an associate's degree as well as a Bachelor's degree in psychology – while working in maintenance and then in a computer-refurbishing program at the correctional facility. According to staff there, Yaklich was a hard and industrious worker, even volunteering her time as a member of the Fire Response Team, comprised of prisoners trained in firefighting and first aid.

Yaklich has also volunteered with several programs that support victims of abuse, earning high praise from her Department of Corrections supervisors regarding the effectiveness of her work with young people. She encourages victims of domestic abuse to seek support from therapy groups to find the strength to break away from an abusive partner – to learn how to stay away emotionally and physically.

"Educating ourselves about the issues and statistics relative to domestic violence will help us pass this information on to the next generation," Yaklich said. "Our children need to learn that they have the right to safe and abuse-free lives."

COLD HEARTED BITCH : THE TRUE STORY OF LYNN TURNER

KELLY COBB

The only thing that Lynn Turner loved more than a man in uniform was the act of killing one.

A certified cop killer, she would go on to marry and murder two different police officers in two different counties.

It started in 1995 when her husband Glenn Turner came into an emergency room claiming he was "sick with the flu." He would die one day later.

The same affliction would befall her common-law-husband, Randy Thompson.

Despite the parallels between the two cases, police still had difficulty proving the case. Lynn Thompson had failed to become a police officer years earlier and made a vow to "outsmart" the people who rejected her by committing the perfect murder.

This is how she tried to do it.

Julia Lynn was given up for adoption at birth and taken in by the Womack family on July 13th, 1968. Her adopted mother, Helen, was a legal secretary and the couple spoiled Lynn as much as they could. They bought her the most expensive toys and clothes they could afford. Unfortunately, the Womacks divorced when she was five and Helen would take full custody of Lynn. Helen would remarry but Lynn did not get along with her new step-father, D.L. Gregory.

As Lynn reached her teen years, she got caught up in drugs. The addiction soon got out of control and she was sent to a drug rehabilitation clinic in Atlanta.

Lynn would eventually graduate high school and begin working as a police dispatcher in addition to having a civilian position working with an undercover narcotic unit in Chattanooga. Lynn loved the police and firefighter culture, hanging out with them outside of work.

"She used to drive around in a Camaro," forensic psychologist Paula Orange said. "She wore tight pants and blouses, showing off her curvaceous bust. She also spent a lot of money she didn't have. For her, it was all about the appearance of being someone better than what she really was."

She would go to bars, hot tubs and shoot pool with the various men in uniform. One night, she would meet Cobb County police officer Glenn Turner at a house party in suburban Atlanta.

"It started out as a one night stand," Orange said. "Unfortunately for Glenn, it didn't stay that way. He became obsessed with the sexy Lynn and fell into her web. Lynn was not the most attractive girl that Glenn had come across. There were women in his church that were better looking than she was. But she had a way of dialing into what a man wanted."

Lynn was smitten with Glenn and began pursuing him aggressively. She would buy him exotic snakeskin cowboy boots as a gift coupled with tickets to baseball and NASCAR. Glenn's friends were suspicious as Glenn was not exactly a ladies man. He had a spare tire and was nicknamed "Buddha" because of jowly appearance.

"I'm sure Glenn didn't think that he could get that type of woman," Roswell detective Sylvia Browning said. "He felt she wasn't in his league and that she was a great catch."

"Glenn grew up in a Christian culture," Orange said. "He was taught to respect and court women. Then along comes Lynn and he does not have to do any of that. She's doing all the work. She does all of the seducing and all of the courting. He was the one swept off his feet."

Glenn's group of police friends (who referred to themselves as the "Rat Pack"), noticed that Lynn was also a big spender.

They had her pegged as a gold-digger but if Glenn was happy they would go along with it.

"She flirted with everybody," Glenn's friend Donald Cawthon said. "She often seemed to need to be the center of attention."

She also had a temper to go along with her flirtatious nature.

"She had an ability to go from being sweet to being hateful within seconds," Glenn's sister, Linda Hardy said.

Both his sister and family alike thought that the couple had very little in common aside from being NASCAR fans. They would go to the races together and Glenn would buy Lynn a pace car similar to the one they used at the Dayton 500.

BIGGER DREAMS

Lynn was described as someone who wanted a champagne diet on a beer budget. She didn't like being a "mere dispatcher" and had bigger dreams of better status. She wanted to be looked at as a "somebody" rather than another working class stiff. Lynn told Glenn of her desire to become a police officer and quit her dispatcher job.

"She wanted entrance into that clique," Orange said. "To be fully accepted. I think Lynn always felt like an outsider as more and more female officers entered the ranks."

Lynn was physically fit and she easily passed the physical tests on the police officer exam. She would fail the psychological exam, however. This failure would prove devastating to her psyche.

She did not want to go back to work as a dispatcher, telling Glenn that she felt it was "humiliating" after she had tried to go out for a police officer and failed. She then began snooping around the city for a more prestigious job but nothing came up. Faced with no other options, Lynn began calling in sick frequently for her dispatch job.

While on the job, her flirting with other officers did not stop. His brothers in blue didn't follow up on Lynn's offer out of respect for Glenn who was well-liked on the force. Still, his fellow officers worried about him as he showed up to work one day to show off an expensive engagement ring he had purchased. The ring was more than he could afford on his cop's salary but he bought it anyway, determined to propose to Lynn on Christmas day.

"He pulled out that little ring box, and I said, 'Oh, you have lost your damn mind,'" Cawthon said.

Lynn would agree to the marriage and they would move in together with a wedding targeted for August of 1993. Before the marriage vows were consummated, however, Lynn convinced Glenn to name her as the beneficiary on his insurance policies. It took some prodding and cajoling but he finally relented.

Word got back to his friends about the arrangement and they were all shocked.

They believed Glenn should have known better as Lynn was already in a ton of debt. She had a mortgage and car payment that nearly exceeded her monthly pay as a dispatcher. She was also saddled with penalty charges on her over-the-limit spending on both her credit cards and checking account.

She was looking for a meal ticket and Glenn was all too eager to provide.

WEDDING DAY & HONEYMOON

Glenn's family and friends all looked ill at ease at the wedding.

"Lynn is a strange girl," Glenn's mother Kathy said.

During the ceremony, the couple was unable to light the unity candle. Glenn's brother James thought that it would be a portent of things to come.

"I feel like I'm more at a funeral than a wedding," James said during his awkward speech as best man. "I don't see this working out, but I hope for the best."

Glenn's friends' began taking bets on how long their friend would last.

Lynn's gold-digger ways would manifest themselves immediately after the wedding vows were exchanged. She chastised Glenn for booking a family cruise instead of the "luxury one". Their sex life wasn't much better as Glenn confided to his friends that Lynn had "female problems" and that their once robust sex life had grounded to a halt.

Six months into their marriage, the two began sleeping in separate bedrooms.

"Despite being in law enforcement and having street smarts," Orange said "Glenn seemed blind to all of the warning signs going on around him. Rather than take a step back and say, 'there is something wrong here', he blamed himself for all of their problems. He thought by catering to her every whim that she would see the light and try to make things work. He didn't have the life experience with women to realize that tactic does not work."

"He'd call her while we were working and say, 'Hey, can I bring you something to eat?'" fellow officer David Dunkerton said. "Most of the time she was downright rude to him. He'd hang up and say, 'Why do I even bother?'"

LET THE SPENDING BEGIN

Lynn acted as if she didn't have a care in the world. She financed a Datsun 240Z and began booking exotic vacations. Glenn could not keep up. He took an extra job as a gas station attendant just to keep up with Lynn's spending.

He bought nothing for himself.

"Lynn put him on a budget the last year of his life," Glenn's sister Linda said. "Twenty bucks a week."

After a few months, Glenn became convinced that Lynn would never see the light. Glenn mentioned divorce and then Lynn threatened to "shoot him with his own gun."

Fearing for his own safety, Glenn again confided in longtime partner Dunkerton. He told his friend that if anything happened to him, to immediately look at Lynn.

Lynn would go back and forth between her home in Cobb County with Glenn and her original hometown of Cumming, Georgia. It was there she would begin an affair with Randy Thompson, a Forsyth County firefighter. Glenn did not know of Lynn's infidelity but was already making arrangements for a divorce.

But before he could file papers he would inexplicably fall ill. On March 2nd, 1995 he was transported to the emergency room complaining of the "flu."

The staff treated him over the course of a few hours and he left the facility feeling better.

But when Lynn came home the next day, she found him dead in his bed.

The coroner chalked Glenn's death to "natural causes due to an irregular heartbeat."

She would collect over $150,000 from her husband's life insurance and receive his pension from the police department.

MOVING ON UP

Glenn's mother, Kathy, was suspicious about her son's death. Glenn was a healthy young man with no health issues and only thirty-one years old. He could not have died from "natural causes."

She looked at the autopsy report and wanted to know what the green substance was in Glenn's stomach at the time of his death. She thought it could be the Jell-O that Lynn fed him and wanted a further examination.

She was then told that further testing could be done but only by an outside agency which would cost a few thousand dollars.

Kathy, who worked as a house cleaner, did not have that kind of money and her questions went unanswered.

Glenn's fellow Rat Pack friends had their suspicions as well, commenting on how Lynn didn't shed one tear at his funeral.

"I've got to get the hell out of here," Lynn said before walking out hand-in-hand with another police officer.

Four days later, unknown to Glenn's family and friends, Lynn moved in with her lover, Randy Thompson.

Randy did not know that Lynn was married. They met through a mutual friend and hit it off. She plied him with gifts, just as she did Glenn, and took him on a luxury cruise.

"I couldn't understand why she was chasing Randy the way she was," Randy's mother, Nita Thompson said. "At first, he wasn't interested. But she was very, very persistent. She told all of us, including Randy, that she was divorced."

Randy Thompson had one daughter and worked as a Forsyth County Sheriff deputy when he first met Lynn. He would later achieve his lifelong dream of becoming a firefighter.

He had a similar personality to Glenn in that he was a jolly and kind man who deferred to women.

"He fit her archetype," Orange said. "She had the ability to target men that she knew she could win over with gifts and attention. Men who were unused to a woman pursuing them. Then once they were in her web she would flip the script. They would become the ones catering to her."

After Lynn won over Randy, she began working on his family. During their first Christmas together she splurged and bought members of his family extravagant gifts.

"She bought us all kinds of stuff," Nita Thompson said. "A CD and stereo combined. Gifts for my daughters. We had just met her and she's buying us all this extravagant stuff."

Lynn knew how to manipulate. It all came naturally to her. From the moment she was born, she herself was showered with gifts and knew how it could often be a method to get people to lower their guard. Even Thompson's mother Nita would later concede that she thought Lynn was a good mother to the children she would bear with her son.

SECOND TIME IS A CHARM

Lynn treated Randy better than she treated Glenn...at least in the beginning of their relationship.

"She bought all of this new stuff," Nita Thompson said. "She bought him a new car. Bought all kinds of stuff and finally, I asked her 'How can you afford all this?' and she said it was from an inheritance from her grandmother."

But the truth was she was purchasing all of these items from collecting Glenn's life insurance. These purchases would include a large ranch style home in Cumming, Georgia.

"Lynn had to have the best in life," Orange said. "She needed the biggest home, the flashiest car. Next came the children. She was fashioning the life that she wanted. If someone got in the way of that, watch out."

In January of 1996 , Lynn would give birth to a daughter, Amber. A year later, she would bear Randy another child, a boy named Randy.

Randy wanted to marry Lynn but she refused. He went so far as to give her an engagement ring but she never wore it. Her refusal to wear the ring hurt him a lot.

Lynn didn't want to marry Randy as she would become ineligible for Glenn's pension. But, true to form, she convinced Randy to add her as the beneficiary of his life insurance policy. He reluctantly agreed to the request and then she prodded him to increase the policy amount from $100,000 to $200,000.

Randy consented to the increase but then saw Lynn's behavior worsen. The two would fight on a regular basis and on one occasion Randy punched her in the mouth. She charged him with battery and he was fined $400 with ten months probation.

"Lynn specialized in finding emotionally fragile men," Orange said. "She found one in Randy who suffered from alcoholism after his first marriage ended. She knew how to play him and reportedly did so on a regular basis, making his life miserable."

Randy would drink heavily and took an overdose of pills during his time with Lynn. His family and friends thought he did it to get Lynn's attention. Friends would comment that their relationship seemed to work together when Randy "needed" her. Lynn needed Randy to be reliant on her for his emotional needs. When she didn't get it, the couple would fight.

"Randy had his own issues," Orange said. "These issues dated back to his first marriage. When he married Lynn, he tried to commit suicide a few times. But these looked to be simply attention-getting gestures. She had abused him emotionally to the point where he felt it necessary to try and kill himself to get her to be nice to him. So she had the power in the relationship. He was this big, bear of a man. An intimidating looking former sheriff and firefighter. But this petite woman had more power over him."

In 1999, just like Glenn, Randy would have enough and leave Lynn.

"I'm leaving for my own sanity," Randy told a friend.

His conscience got to him quickly over a few weeks. He decided he wanted to reconcile just for the sake of the children. They were only five and two years old at the time.

"It was difficult for Randy to leave the kids," Orange said. "It just broke the man's heart. He had to leave the kids and then negotiate with the cold-hearted Lynn to see them again. She was breaking him down mentally."

"If he (Randy) did the slightest thing to make her mad," Nita Thompson said. "She wouldn't let him see them (the children)."

Randy also began experiencing health problems. He suffered from a staph infection and had a stent inserted near his heart. Still, he recovered and came out of his illness with a renewed hope that things could be reconciled.

Lynn agreed to Randy's request to have a family dinner at the Longhorn Steakhouse in town.

They would then go back to Lynn's house for dessert but Randy would not spend the night.

"I asked him how things went," Nita Thompson said. "And he said 'not well.'"

Days later, Randy began to experience several abdominal pain and vomiting. He went to the emergency room but was later discharged home.

In his apartment alone, he telephoned his firefighter friend, Paul Adams.

Adams arrived to find the entire apartment a veritable mess. There was overturned furniture and various items on the floor.

Randy was hysterical.

"Do you think I'm going to die?" Randy asked.

The following morning, another firefighter friend, Barry Head, would find Randy dead.

He had been complaining of flu symptoms and had visited the emergency room earlier in the day. Similar to Glenn, he had extreme abdominal pain and was vomiting. The hospital released him into Lynn's care.

"She had 'nursed' him in the same way she had 'nursed' Glenn," Orange said. "She gave him tea and soup. Then some Jell-O. She had poisoned all of his food, however."

Randy did not show up for work the day after having 'dessert' with Lynn. His co-workers became worried.

"Several of his friends called," Randy's mother, Nita Thompson said. "And several of his friends went over to see why he wasn't answering his phone calls."

Randy's firefighter friends arrived at his home, peering through the window blinds. They could see Randy on the couch appearing to be asleep. They knocked and knocked to no avail.

Worried, they kicked the door down, hoping to revive their friend.

But Randy had been dead for hours.

He was only thirty-two years old.

"He and I were very close," Nita Thompson said. "He was my first-born and my only son."

Lynn showed no emotion when told of Randy's death. Her friends chalked up it to her "stuffing" her emotions as she could often come across as a "cold fish."

"Lynn was a psychopath who could only display a limited amount of emotions," Orange said. "She could fake happiness. But she couldn't fake sorrow. She couldn't feel it and she didn't know how to fake it, unlike some other female killers."

A BLACK WIDOW BITES

The coroner would again write off Thompson's death as "natural causes due to an irregular heartbeat."

The day before his funeral, Lynn contacted Randy's insurance company. She tossed the phone at the wall in anger when she found out that Randy's policy had been canceled as he had not been paying the premiums.

She instead only collected $36,000.

Soon, however, she would have other things to worry about. The parallels between Randy's and Glenn's death were too similar not to be ignored. Someone had to notice something...

That someone was Mike Archer, Glenn's former sergeant. He got in touch with Glenn's mother and vowed justice. His mother told him that she knew the truth all along but didn't know how to proceed.

Armed with the new information about Randy's death, the Rat Pack began a phone campaign to alert authorities of their suspicions about Lynn.

News media got hold of the story and began referring to Lynn as the "messenger of death" and a "black widow."

Randy Thompson's mother would receive a sympathy letter from Glenn Turner's mother saying that her son died of the same thing. Neither mother knew that both of their sons were intimately involved with Lynn Turner. The two began to exchange notes about what their sons had gone through and immediately put two and two together.

Lynn Turner had killed their sons. Not the flu.

A blood test was done on Thompson which would reveal the ethylene glycol based anti-freeze in his system.

"She had poured anti-freeze into his Jell-O," Orange said. "The anti-freeze was both colorless and odorless. If anything, it had a sweet taste. It would blend right in with his Jell-O, tea or soup. All she needed was about a third of a cup to poison the men. It would crystallize in their liver and cause a very painful death."

Further investigation would reveal that Lynn visited a local animal shelter, asking off-hand about what type of poison they used to put animals down.

"They told her about the 'purple liquid' they used to put down strays," Orange said. "Lynn inquired further and was told that the same chemicals existed in anti-freeze."

The police knew they were onto to something after they found the anti-freeze in Thompson's system. They then exhumed Glenn's body and found the exact same substance in his kidneys.

Crime scene photos from Glenn Turner's death would have a picture taken in the garage where the anti-freeze was visible.

"No one put two and two together at the time," Orange said. "To them, it was just a container of anti-freeze on the shelf in the garage. A typical sight."

ARREST AND CONVICTION

Lynn would be arrested for Glenn's murder ten months after she killed Randy. She would sit and listen with a bored facial expression as the prosecution built their case against her. Outside the courtroom, however, she would joke and laugh with reporters, boasting that she would go free.

"Lynn learned how to fake certain emotions," Orange said. "She is one of those people that I think are born bad. She didn't do what she did solely because of the money with the life insurance or what not. There was something else at play, especially when she was refused entry into the police force. She wanted to prove how much smarter she was than them. She truly believed that."

"She would have gotten away with the first murder. But she did it twice. But for the Thompson murder, she would have gotten away with murdering Glenn. God knows what else she did in her life to warrant her arrogance. She was never caught for anything until the second murder."

Lynn would be tried for Glenn's murder in 2004 and be found guilty. She would again go to trial in 2007 for Randy's murder and be convicted.

Lynn would be sentenced to life in prison without parole, serving out her time at the Metro State Prison in Georgia.

On August 30th, 2010, Lynn was found "unresponsive" in her jail cell and could not be revived. Her death would be ruled a suicide. She had accumulated enough of her blood-pressure medication pills to ingest and she overdosed.

Lynn's mother, Helen, visited her the previous Sunday and had her own suspicions on what happened to her daughter. Helen said that she feared for her daughter's safety as she alluded to being threatened by other inmates.

"As I started to leave," Helen recalled. "She said, 'Momma, those girls are going to get me. I just know they will.'"

An autopsy would later reveal no signs of foul play.

Glenn's friends still gather each year at his grave.

BLACK WIDOW TILLIE KLIMEK

CARA DAVIDSON

Ottilie "Tillie" Klimek—born Ottilie Gburek—was a Polish American serial killer who was active in Chicago during the early 1900s. She allegedly murdered between six and 20 individuals by poisoning them with arsenic. Additional victims included her other husbands, a boyfriend, relatives and various neighbors with help of her cousin Nellie Koulik.

Klimek is purported to have experienced precognitive dreams which predicted her victims' actual dates of deaths; however, in reality, she was simply "scheduling" them as there is no historic evidence in any of the literature that she had any psychic gifts or precognition skills. While Klimek was arrested after nearly poisoning her last husband Joseph Klimek—for which she was tried, convicted, and given a life sentence—she was only convicted of one murder; that of her third husband, Frank Kupszcyk. She was sentenced to life in prison in 1923 and subsequently died on 20 November 1936.

Early Life

Ottilie "Tillie" Klimek was born Ottilie Gburek in 1876 in Poland. When she was about a year old, her parents immigrated with her to the United States along with many eastern European lower classes who were among the first immigrants who left their homelands in search of a better life in the United States. The Gbureks settled in the north side Chicago neighborhood dubbed "Little Poland." At the time, Chicago boasted the second-largest Polish population in the world, after Warsaw, Poland. The families who settled in Little Poland were largely law-abiding and God-fearing people so when word of Klimek's later activities became known even her own people looked at her with disdain.

While there is scant information on much of Klimek's early life until her teenage years when she first married, there is ample evidence in the literature that she was an amazing cook. In fact, her special "stew" was her claim to fame, in more ways than one. Another of Klimek's special "gifts" was her self-proclaimed psychic ability that enabled her to accurately "predict" the deaths of certain people and animals. She began by predicting the demise of neighborhood pets which were almost always accurate. She then "predicted" the death of all of her husbands, a boyfriend, several relatives with whom she had quarreled or who had otherwise done her wrong.

Absent other early biological data, it is known that Klimek married her first husband, John Mitkiewicz, in 1890, when she was just 14 years of age. He died in 1914 after a relatively short illness and his death certificate states that he died from a heart attack.

Shortly after collecting her life insurance check from her husband's death, Klimek married Joseph Ruskowski, whom she had met through a matchmaker. He would pass away a mere three months later and Tillie was on the lookout for another relationship.

This time the unlucky fellow was Joseph Guszkowski who is listed as a boyfriend who allegedly jilted her; however, in some accounts he is listed as one of Klimek's husbands, so the legal nature of their relationship is not conclusive. Guszkowski would die in 1914 as well. At his funeral Klimek acted wholly surprised that she had such bad luck with men and also cursed her "ominous dreams" in front of everyone. Whether her melodramatic display actually convinced others that she truly felt cursed and tragic is up for speculation.

Klimek then her wed third husband, Frank Kupszcyk. The unhappily-married couple lived in an apartment at 924 N. Winchester; the same apartment in which she had resided with Joseph Guszkowski.

On 25 April 1921, a mere two years after they exchanged their vows, Frank died shortly after Klimek "foretold" his death from one of her premonitions and within a year—in true grieving-widow form—Klimek was in another relationship.

Over the warnings and protestations of his family and friends, Joseph Klimek—who had attended Frank's funeral for some reason not fully explained in the literature except, perhaps, to get close to the newly-single Klimek—decided to marry the widow with the troubling reputation. The couple wed in 1921 and resided at 1453 Tell Place (later renamed Thomas Street). When Joseph became sick, the doctors suspected arsenic poisoning and subsequent medical tests confirmed their suspicions. Thankfully, Joseph survived and his wife was arrested for attempted murder. The full extent of her murderous ways would soon be made public.

The Crimes

Klimek was frequently seen as a psychic by her neighbors and others in Chicago as her "uncanny talent" of foreseeing the exact dates of deaths for her five husbands—only four actually perished at her hand—as well as other neighbors was seen as both astounding and a little bit alarming because nobody wanted to know when they were supposed to die.

Klimek's "talent", however, would soon be revealed as bogus, she knew damn well when these people would die because she would be the one to kill them. Her murderous spree began in 1914 and ended in 1922 when she was arrested for the attempted murder of her last husband Joseph Klimek.

Called a "Black Widow", Klimek started down this macabre road rather late in life when compared to other well-known black widows. She was in her mid-30's when she claimed her first victim—her first husband. Experts alleged that this is an age at which most husband-killing women stop their activities.

John Mitkiewicz

In January 1914, Klimek "predicted" the death of her long-time husband, John Mitkiewicz, whom she had married in 1890. Klimek allegedly told a friend that she dreamt that she had discovered his corpse on a specific date a few weeks in the future and, of course, acted worried about the "news." When John fell sick on that exact day and died later that night, her friend was awestruck.

Klimek to have sprinted to the insurance office to collect the $1,000 proceeds upon his death. Eyebrows were not raised at this time because, after all, people died, wives inherited life insurance monies, and, ultimately, life went on.

But post-exhumation investigation would reveal that John had been poisoned with a lethal amount of arsenic.

Many assert that this first murder was one of convenience and profit that quickly became a way for Klimek to make a living by collecting life insurance payments and exact revenge on those she believed had wronged her.

John Ruskowski

Klimek did not remain a widow for long. A mere two months later, she married John Ruskowski, a laborer who quickly became the subject of one of Klimek's precognitive dreams. Whereas neighbors—and John himself—initially laughed at her predictions and chalked them up to nonsense, when he died on the stated date in May 1914, they became true believers.

Klimek received approximately $1,200 in cash and just over $700 in life insurance funds from his death. Again, his death did not elicit much cause for alarm at the time.

Joseph Guszkowski

Her next victim would be Joseph Guszkowski, whose relationship with Klimek differs depending upon the account one reads. In most reports, Joseph is listed as a boyfriend who allegedly jilted Klimek which, in turn, spurred her into action; while in other accounts John is stated to have been her fourth husband. Regardless of the actual relationship, the outcome did not change.

Klimek told Joseph—albeit in a roundabout way—that her previous husbands did not, exactly, perish from natural causes but that she had deliberately poisoned them with arsenic.

Scared shitless, Joseph sought to end their relationship. Klimek then threatened to bring Joseph to justice under the Mann Act; a piece of 1920s legislation that initially sought to stop interstate commerce of women for the purpose of sexual activity. Joseph became angrier and threatened to tell authorities about Klimek's "arsenic tendencies." This proved to be a very bad move when Klimek "foretold" his death which, not surprisingly, reached fruition exactly when she said it would.

Frank Kupszcyk

Klimek married third husband Frank Kupszcyk in 1919 and he grew ill after consuming his wife's delicious vegetable soup with the one extra ingredient: arsenic. As Frank got sicker and sicker, Klimek would say things to her neighbors that her current husband "would not live long" and that he only had "two inches to live." She even taunted Frank to his face by telling him, "It won't be long now," and "You'll be dying soon."

Klimek sewed her own mourning hat—which she later wore at his funeral and at her trial—while sitting beside her husband as he was suffering on his deathbed. Klimek also had the audacity to ask her landlady for permission to store a coffin in the building's basement that she had purchased on sale for $30.

Frank eventually died in 1921. Klimek played loud and cheerful dance music on a phonograph in the same room and celebrated upon his death. At his service, Klimek reached into her dead husband's coffin to grab his ear and shouted, "You devil, you won't get up anymore!"

Klimek was listed as the sole beneficiary on her late husband's life insurance policy, and ultimately collected $675 from it.

It was during this time that Klimek was gaining notoriety with many wondering how she was able to attract husbands given the ominous ends of those who came before. Also, by this point, others in the community had started avoiding Klimek in public so as not to hear predictions about their own deaths.

Joseph Klimek

Klimek's last husband Joseph Klimek—who married the black widow in 1921 even after being warned by friends and families—also became ill after they had been married for a short time. Klimek had spoken to her cousin Nellie Sturmer Koulik—who also "had a dead husband under her belt"—and confided in her that her latest marriage was not all rosy and that she was, in fact, sick and tired of her husband. When Nellie suggested divorce, Klimek said, "I will get rid of him some other way" to which Nellie allegedly gave her cousin a knowing look and a "goodly portion" of rat poison called "Rough on Rats" that was comprised of arsenic and easy to purchase at that time. Ironically, the slogan for the poison was "Don't die in the house."

Naturally, Joseph fell ill with some of the classic symptoms of arsenic poisoning: stiff legs and garlic-smelling breath.

Joseph's brother John became quite suspicious at his brother's rapid-onset illness and the fact that his sister-in-law didn't seem too worried. Compounding the problem was that two of Joseph's pet dogs had also recently died abruptly and under strange circumstances. John phoned his own doctor to come to the Klimek's residence to examine Joseph and the family physician immediately suspected that the sick man was suffering from arsenic poisoning. They took Joseph to the hospital and saved his life. After running several tests, this diagnosis was later confirmed.

While Joseph survived, he did have to spend a grueling three months in the hospital recuperating.

Klimek was subsequently arrested on 26 October 1922, for the attempted murder of her husband Joseph. She told the arresting officer that, "The next one I want to cook a dinner for is you. You made all my trouble."

Other Victims

One of Klimek's cousins, Rose Chudzinski, became suspicious of Klimek's psychic "gift" and the tragic ends which befell her men she married. After Klimek had heard the rumors Rose had been spreading, the women quarreled; after which Klimek "predicted" Rose's death. Of course, Rose died in 1919, shortly after this argument which allegedly occurred at the Klimeks' wedding party.

Klimek's and Nellie's other victims include more cousins: 16-year-old Stanley Zakrzewski who died in 1912, 23-year-old cousin Stelle Zakrzewski who died in 1913, and 15-year-old Helen Zakrzewski who died in 1915. Ironically, when her cousins were ill, Klimek had been their primary caretaker and before their deaths, Klimek had allegedly reported she had precognitive dreams in which the cousins were all victims of some sort of deadly plague.

Nellie's infant daughter Sophie Sturmer died in 1917 and her twin brother Ben died one month later. Additionally, Nellie's first husband Wojek Sturmer died in 1918, and arsenic was found in his system after exhumation. Nellie's granddaughter Dorothy Spera died at the tragic age of two. Another of Nellie's sons, John Sturmer, fell ill after his father's death. He recovered; however, convinced that his mother poisoned him as well. Another of Nellie's daughters, Lillian Sturmer, lived at Klimek's house for about a year when she was 13. Although Lillian became deathly ill after eating Klimek's cooking she also survived but suffered serious heart trouble for the rest of her life.

A former boyfriend or sweetheart—or possibly another husband—named "Meyers" went missing in March 1923. Two of Klimek's neighbors—Rose Splitt and Stelle Grantowski—reportedly died after she gave them poisoned candy following an argument they had with Klimek.

Other victims survived. Cousin Nick Micko recovered from his arsenic poisoning after eating one of Klimek's delicious meals, and Bessie Kupszcyk—Klimek's husband Frank's sister-in-law—also fell ill after eating at Klimek's and she, too, recovered.

A neighborhood dog Klimek thought a nuisance who lived on Winchester Street when she had had also perished mysteriously, as had Joseph Klimek's two pet dogs.

In sum, there were 20 suspected victims, 12 of whom had died, seven who were still alive, and one who was missing.

Investigation and Arrest

The year-long investigation yielded much evidence. In addition to a multitude of macabre exhumations, there were also anonymous letters which referenced potential victims and poisoned candy.

It soon became evident that Joseph Klimek's illness was neither mysterious nor isolated. After Klimek's arrest, police received an anonymous letter which led to authorities' exhuming Frank Kupszcyk's body and, voila, the body was chock full of enough arsenic to kill a dozen men. As there was no arsenic in the surrounding soil, investigators had no other conclusion to draw than Frank was poisoned to death.

As would be expected in 1920's Chicago, local newspapers and tabloids had a field day with this information, as well as news that would soon break about additional exhumations.

Another anonymous letter named Klimek's cousin Nellie Koulik as another potential suspect and urged police to look more closely at her. The letter also insisted that police ought to exhume Nellie's first husband—Wojek Strummer—who died in 1918, and to check his body for lethal concentrations of arsenic as the cause of his death. Lo and behold, his body also contained fatal amounts of arsenic. Letters also indicted the two women as aiding and abetting each other's efforts in getting rid of other friends and relatives who had died under similarly mysterious circumstances.

Consequently, Nellie was arrested one week after Klimek.

At some point, police took Klimek to visit her husband in the hospital. Understandably, he was angry, upset, curious, and, thus, full of questions; however, she often replied with "I don't know" or admonished her husband to not bother her anymore about such trivial matters. It is reported that at one point Klimek overhead him asking a nurse for some water to which she replied that if he continued to be a troublemaker to just hit him over the head with a two-by-four. Before leaving, Klimek kissed her husband, said action baffling everyone given her demeanor toward him as well as the curious statements she had made to hospital staff.

While preparations were being made to exhume Klimek's first couple of husbands, two of her cousins arrived and requested that police exhume four additional bodies; those of three siblings who died under mysterious conditions after having eaten at Klimek's house and that Klimek had been angry with their mother, not to mention that she had had her precognitive dreams about them, as well as another cousin with whom Klimek had argued.

Police also learned about Joseph Guszkowski—Klimek's former boyfriend/husband—who also died under mysterious circumstances. Thus, additional exhumation orders were ordered and processed and both Klimek and Nellie were formally charged with murder: Klimek for Frank Kupszcyk, and Nellie for her first husband Wojek Strummer. However, after following the all of the clues and trails from the anonymous letters and other involved parties' recommendations, detectives found three more graves; very small ones belonging to Nellie's twin babies and her granddaughter.

Nellie had given birth to her twins—Sophie and Ben Sturmer—while still married to Wojek; however, as she was having an affair with her future second husband, Albert Koulik, at the same time, Wojek denied that he was the twins' biological father. Of course, Nellie did not take this refusal very well. Consequently, one twin, Sophie, died at eight months of age and the other, Ben, a month later. The third dead child was Nellie's two-year-old granddaughter, Dorothy Spera, who she also poisoned because Nellie's daughter (the child's mother) was critical of the way Nellie lived and the choices she had made. When the poor child fell ill, Nellie insisted on caring for her. Subsequently, the baby's feet and face swelled from the abundance of arsenic in her body and she eventually died in her grandmother's care.

Additional victims included other relatives, friends, and neighbors who had all eaten at Klimek's or Nellie's at some point and had fallen ill shortly thereafter.

Nellie's sister Cornelia was also arrested because Cornelia's son-in-law suspected that she was poisoning him by lacing his moonshine with arsenic.

Word got out that Klimek was likely not a singular serial killer but some sort of "high priestess of a Bluebeard clique" within the Little Poland, Chicago neighborhood. Assistant State Attorney W.F. McLaughlin had it in for Klimek from the get-go and made no bones about it. Many have suggested that he sought some sort of professional immortality he believed he could achieve through this case. Thus, he demonstrated considerable melodrama and exaggeration when he referred to the alleged Bluebeard clique as "the most astounding wholesale poisoning plot ever uncovered" as well as "the most amazing death plot in recent criminal history." This widespread accusation caused other neighborhood women to be arrested; however, they were subsequently released when the whole concept of such as clique was dispelled.

As for Klimek, however, McLaughlin wanted blood and vehemently sought the death penalty.

While in custody, Nellie's English-speaking capacity diminished considerably. She was also reported as being relatively happy and good natured given the situation—even allowing reporters to photograph her once she had fixed her hair, of course; however, she did have a reputation for hysterics, particularly in response to her cousin's poor choice and timing of various gallows humor. Oftentimes Klimek would convince Nellie that the authorities were on their way and that she was to be hanged and the naïve Nellie often believed her cousin's statements.

Conversely, Klimek, while in custody, was insolent, quiet, controlled, and icy—almost robot-like in her demeanor and lack of emotion. The only reactions she ever displayed was when she repeatedly—and vehemently—denied killing anyone. She was also rather emotional when she claimed that everyone was "picking on" and "making eyes" at her.

Despite her denials, there was ample physical evidence and Klimek's protestations of innocence were not believed by anyone, especially her husband Joseph.

Trial

The trial commenced on 27 February 1923, against the woman known as "Mrs. Bluebeard" and "The Polish Borgia"; the latter in reference to the infamous Borgia family of 15th- and 16th-century Spain whose members were noted for several heinous crimes including murder by arsenic poisoning.

Joseph Klimek was to be McLaughlin's star witness in the proceedings against his wife, the alleged leader of some heinous Bluebeard clique and poisoner of 20 people, in a trial in which State Attorney McLaughlin was enthusiastically seeking the death penalty. If successful, such would set a new precedent as the state of Illinois had never executed a woman and this is likely why McLaughlin was so passionate about finding Klimek guilty. So passionate, in fact, that he beseeched the jury throughout the entire proceedings to step it up and finally sentence a woman to death. And Klimek was his perfect woman—a husband-killer four times over.

Medical experts testified that Joseph experienced acute paralysis by the covert, prolonged, and regular introduction of arsenic into his food. As a result, he had lost the use of his legs due to the paralytic property of arsenic.

Joseph testified that after his wife talked him into purchasing more life insurance, her meals began to taste a bit "queer" but he never in a million years suspected that she was slowly killing him.

Klimek, in her own behalf, was adamant that she did not murder her husbands. She claimed that Frank died from alcohol poisoning;

saying this while wearing the death hat she had sewn while he lay dying. She also insisted that she loved her husbands deeply and they loved her as well. She also questioned the fuss made over the fact that people die all the time. However, by the end of the trial—and listening to the medical examiner's testimony that arsenic was, indeed, found in all of her husband's systems—her stoic façade had begun to crumble and, for the first time, Tillie Klimek looked somewhat anxious.

During the trial, psychiatrists testified about evaluations they had conducted while the women were awaiting trial. In their analyses, they alleged that both women had some type of mental defect and likely suffered from dementia praecox; a chronic and deteriorating psychotic disorder that causes rapid cognitive disintegration and that typically manifests itself in late adolescence or young adulthood. The women had also been assessed as having the intelligence of an 11-year-old child. This particularly interested the presiding judge because he knew that one of Nellie's sons had already been declared to be feeble-minded several years ago and the judge was a firm believer in genetics and an advocate of eugenics. Thus, he was of the mindset that if individuals were determined to be mentally inferior and prone to criminality then fieldworkers and police officers could keep their eyes on their relatives as they, in his mind, had a greater propensity for deviance as well. Such as mindset is a scary thing as history is rife with individuals with similar ideas who have committed horrible atrocities on those determined to be "lesser" people.

One critic of the psychological reports and tests asserts that because neither Klimek nor Nellie spoke perfect English that there was a great likelihood that they did not understand some of the questions or other aspects of the evaluation and this could have accounted for the results. Thus, had they been evaluated in their native language—or even had a translator provided—then, perhaps, the results would have been different because Klimek demonstrated, on many occasions, that she was extremely smart and cunning.

The trial was covered by many of the new wave of Chicago's "girl reporters" including Genevieve Forbes who was one of the country's pioneers with respect to females working the crime beat news. During that era, a female crime reporter was an anomaly. Genevieve interviewed Joseph in the hospital, she contacted Klimek's troubled parents, and she even tried to interview the stoic Klimek herself who Genevieve could not get to lower her guard even a tiny bit. Genevieve's analyses were oftentimes brutal and unforgiving but she also had a reputation for being relatively fair. Thus, her recognition that Klimek was, indeed, a vengeful, cunning, and dangerous woman rang true; as did her assessment that Nellie really posed little threat.

The public's perception of Klimek did not help matters much. Genevieve described the murderess as "a fat, squat Polish peasant woman", looking considerably older than her 40-something years, with "a lumpy figure, capacious hands and feet", and dull hair pulled back into a severe bun at the back of her head. Yet, despite the brutally honest and unflattering description, Genevieve did acknowledge Klimek's intelligence and dispelled aspects of the psychiatric testimony. Genevieve also wrote that because Klimek was neither beautiful nor "flawlessly American" she could not escape the widespread belief that she was stupid or slow or—as immigrants were commonly known at that time—a lowly peasant.

Other "journalists" reported that, unlike other women who killed their husbands and had been acquitted (think Kander and Ebb's epic play *Chicago* set during this era), Klimek, as mentioned, was neither beautiful nor charming. She also spoke poor English despite having lived in Chicago for pretty much her entire life. In other words, Klimek did not abide the established "rules" of the 1920's Chicago husband-murdering "game" which necessitated flirting, getting all dolled up, and sobbing demurely to elicit jury and judge favor or sympathy culminating in an acquittal. Thus, her trial evolved into a circus of sorts with the judge having to—on many occasions—threaten the courtroom with, "This is not a theater!"

While denying her responsibility, overtly denouncing her special psychic gift, and attempts to elicit sympathy and compassion for her bad luck with the men in her life, Klimek was confident that she would not be executed. In fact, she was correct. While the state did not have to enforce the death penalty as she was sentenced to life in prison without parole, the state did keep its promise to keep her locked up for the rest of her life.

Her trial concluded in March when she was found guilty of Frank's murder and she was sentenced to life in prison. At the time this was the harshest sentence ever given to a female defendant in the history of Cook County.

One interesting but understandable stipulation of her sentence was that she never be permitted to cook for the other inmates.

Whereas the public was initially interested in Klimek even though she wasn't as young and attractive as other murderesses over which the public would fawn, the public quickly lost interest in Chicago's latest husband killer. At the time, a female murderer was noteworthy; however, absent an equally noteworthy backstory—or stunning beauty—the once spectacular headline simply vanished from the public's consciousness.

Cousin Nellie's tedious year in prison alongside her unrepentant cousin culminated in her acquittal. Even though her own children had testified against her, the jury found her not guilty of giving Klimek the rat poison which killed Frank. After the acquittal, McLaughlin dropped the murder charge—even though her husband's body showed a high level of arsenic—against her for several reasons. First, with Klimek convicted and sentenced to life in prison, the whole idea of the Bluebeard clique lost its appeal. Secondly, other murderesses were taking over the front page and, as a result, the public's consciousness.

Klimek died in prison on 20 November 1936. Reports cite a heart attack as her cause of death.

Aftermath

Much reference is made to Klimek's use of poison throughout her murder spree. Poison is a common method for murder for women, according to several experts. This is likely because it enables killers to get close to their victims while also deciding when and how they would ultimately die. Further, poisoning was a relatively easy murder weapon throughout early history as the forensic knowledge and testing capabilities prevalent today were not as widely known or used. It was only when doctors presumed that Joseph Klimek had been poisoned that they specifically looked for evidence; thus finding arsenic in his system.

Additionally, the criminological literature is rife with theories about female offenders. Elizabeth Yardley and David Wilson, in their book *Female Serial Killers in Social Context* (2015), discuss the multiple motivations of female serial killers. For women, these motivations are largely profit or revenge. Klimek profited from three of her husband's deaths in terms of cashing in their life insurance policies, thus meeting the requirements to be classified as a "Black Widow." Another victim met his demise after allegedly breaking off their relationship so she sought revenge out of anger. The anger-vengeance motive arose again when she killed three of her cousins after having a disagreement with the victims' mother. Revenge was also cited in the death of her cousin Rose Chudzinski as Klimek poisoned Rose's dinner after the two women had an argument. Unlike male serial killers, females typically have multiple motives for their actions and such was, indeed, the case with Tillie Klimek.

Many have written that had Klimek been attractive and demure and everything the public wanted her to be then she would likely have been acquitted even though there was no doubt of her guilt. In fact, at the time, 28 women had been acquitted of murder and, of course, all 28 were attractive. Four others had been found guilty and these four were not attractive. Genevieve Forbes, in a follow-up, retrospective piece on Klimek wrote that she went to prison "because she had never gone to a beauty parlor." Regardless, Klimek adapted well to prison, even reportedly commenting on the delicious prison food.

Joseph Klimek died a few years after the trial. Whereas the cause of death was blamed on tonsillitis, at his autopsy it was discovered that his body was full of arsenic.

Tillie Klimek remains the most prolific female serial killer in Chicago history.

ARSENIC ANNA : THE TRUE STORY OF SERIAL KILLER ANNA MARIE HAHN

DARLA PUGH

"Anna was flat broke. But when she saw a person walking down the street she would think that individual had HER money in their pocket. If she had to kill that person to get HER money, then she would take out her poison and say 'let's get this party started.'" - forensic psychologist Paula Orange

Anna Marie Hahn had a gambling habit.

She indulged her addiction at the horse races and bookie joints throughout Cincinnati in the 1930s. Anna wasn't very good at picking horses, losing time and again while accruing debt.

But it was an addiction had to be fed.

She needed a scheme, a way to acquire money to keep her compulsion satisfied.

Anna Marie Hahn was a clever woman. While walking through her neighborhood of elderly pensioners, the idea came to her like a bolt of lightning.

She would befriend these lonely and pathetic men. Cook them meals, keep them company.

Then she would kill them for profit.

EARLY LIFE

Anna was born Anna Marie Filser on July 7, 1906. She would be the youngest of twelve children born to a well-to-do Catholic family. Nothing in her childhood would suggest that she would eventually become a serial killer. She was never abused sexually or physically.

Nonetheless, she had suffered a few concussions during her childhood years during ice skating, biking and skiing adventures. These head injuries may have attributed to altering her personality as sometimes been the case of some serial killers. Anna also stated that she was a sickly child, suffering from blood poisoning, goiters, and scarlet fever. It is her belief that these instances led to "her mind changing that she could do the things that happened."

As a teen, she had given birth to a son named Oskar out of wedlock. The identity of the father has remained shrouded in mystery to this day although some claim a Viennese doctor had seduced Anna Marie.

She never revealed who the father was as he was a married man who wanted her to abort the child. Anna felt "just like a mountain was falling on top of her, not killing her but just smothering and crushing her."

The pregnancy brought shame to Anna's family. They sent pregnant seventeen-year-old to live with a sister in Holland until the baby was born.

She would return to Germany afterward and remain there for five years. The shame of being a single mom in a conservative, judgmental society would prove to be too much for Anna to bear.

"I could no longer stand those things that people were saying about my misfortune," Anna said. "I was afraid that my son would understand those things. These things were hurting my mother who was caring for my boy."

"Back in the day," Orange said. "Having a baby out of wedlock was the worst thing a woman could do in terms of family legacy. She had humiliated her entire family and was banished to another country. It certainly is an antiquated notion now, to shame a woman for having a child out of wedlock and it has become the norm. In Germany, however, this act was cause for ostracization."

Anna left Germany and arrived in the United States on February 12th, 1929. She had a step-uncle who lived in Cincinnati to whom she had written a year earlier. "I want to come to the United States," she wrote. "I'll repay you if you can lend me money for the trip. I will have little trouble finding work as a housekeeper. Please write back."

Her step-uncle, a seventy-four-year-old retired carpenter, was impressed with Anna's ability to provide for herself once she arrived. She did so well, in fact, that he became suspicious of how she acquired her money.

Oskar would stay behind in Germany with her parents while Anna would live with her now expatriated relatives Max and Anna Doeschel. Growing accustomed to the American way of life, she would meet another German immigrant named Philip Hahn at a dance. Philip was immediately smitten by the blonde and buxom Anna. The courtship did not last very long, a few weeks of dating was all the convincing Philip needed to ask Anna to marry him.

Anna agreed to marry him only on the condition that she be allowed to bring her son from Germany to live with them. Philip consented and the two were married three months after their first meeting on May 5th, 1930, in Buffalo, New York. Two months later, Anna would return to Germany and bring back Oskar who was now six years old. Philip would work as a telegrapher and do his best to now provide his new family.

Wanting a better life for her son, Anna convinced Philip that they should do more. The Depression was in full bloom but that did not stop Anna and Philip from starting their own restaurant and then a bakery. Both ventures would prove to be economic failures. The two soon became bankrupt and were forced to move in with a childhood friend of Anna's father.

Thus marked the continued humiliation of Anna. Branded as a whore by her own family, she was shunned and banished to America where she would suffer the indignity of becoming bankrupt.

GERMANS IN CINCINNATI

There was a sizable German population in Cincinnati and Anna was able to fit in and find friends. She settled in a community called Over The Rhine and she was welcomed with open arms.

She repaid some of these new "friends" by killing them.

"She had it all," author Diane Britt Franklin said. "She knew how to manipulate, steal, poison."

But what prompted her to turn to murder?

The friend of Anna's father had left his home to the Hahn's but they still had a mortgage to pay. Philip lost his job as a telegrapher, a victim of both technology and the Depression. The walls started to close in on the couple as creditors began making threats to take possession of her home.

Anna did not know what else to do.

So she turned to gambling.

Three years into her marriage, Anna was neck-deep in debt because of her gambling habit. She loved the racetracks but could never pick a winner. She would play horses at the Blade, a bookie joint in suburban Elmwood, Ohio then the gaming tables in Newport.

The addiction grew faster than her pocketbook would allow.

She needed money. Fast.

So she found a new way to "earn" money. Unbeknownst to her husband, Anna began plotting ways to pilfer money out of elderly German men who lived in Over the Rhine.

She developed a method typical of male serial killers in that she had a typical victim. Anna thought long and hard about what type of man she should target. The lonely. The old. The German, with whom she would be able to ingratiate herself to.

Anna found an apartment building in Cincinnati that was comprised mostly of older German men.

They were the perfect foil for Anna Hahn. A young and beautiful German woman who spoke their language, they easily fell prey to her charms.

"She went through apartment buildings," Franklin said. "She knocked on doors and asked for old men who were single."

"She developed a method of extracting money from wealthy old people," Orange said. "She would gain access into their homes by offering her services as a nurse. Then she would take their money."

Ernst Kohler was believed to be her first victim. Anna had befriended the lonely German man and he had willed his house to her.

Getting the sense that she was onto something, Anna began "befriending" more elderly men. The next victim was seventy-two-year-old Albert Parker who enlisted Anna's aid as a caretaker. Anna would borrow over $1,000 from Parker and signed an I.O.U for it. After Parker's death, the letter of debt "disappeared."

SETTING THE STAGE

Anna dressed her son in his Sunday's best before they went prospecting for victims. The little boy wore a brown suit with a beige shirt and a derby hat. Anna dressed conservatively, looking like a German mother taking her son out to Sunday School. She wore a gray jacket with a black silk blouse. But Anna made sure that her silver cross necklace stood prominently over her cleavage.

She then knocked on the apartment door of Jacob Wagner and put on her best smile.

Th door creaked open and the elderly German man peered out at them, saying nothing.

"Mr. Wagner," Anna said in a strong German accent. "I'm Anna Marie."

The old man's face brightened with good cheer. He had a young woman to help around the house with chores.

Little did he know that Anna would help herself to his bank account and personal belongings.

"She would take a nickel as easily as a dollar," Franklin said. "She would steal anything in sight."

Jacob Wagner was a retired gardener who only had a few thousand dollars in savings. He was targeted by Anna who would tell his neighbors that she was his niece. The old man became confused, responding back that he had "never heard of her."

"Neither Jacob nor the rest of the community fully realized what a psychopath Anna was," Orange said. "If you had something she wanted, whether it be money or material goods, she would do anything in her power to obtain it. If it meant killing you, so be it."

Anna knew that she only need to apply her feminine wiles on Wagner and he would be putty in her hands. She told the old man that she was an heiress to $15,000 from Germany. She wanted to pool their resources to buy a chicken farm but in the meantime would working around his apartment.

The seventy-eight-year-old Wagner would die on June 3rd, 1937, only months after hiring Anna. The day after the gardener's death, Anna would go to Wagner's bank and present a check that was made payable to her. The bank asked her about the death of Wagner, she had conceded that she had forged the check. Anna would not stop there. She would appear before a probate court with a will that left all of Wagner's property to her.

She had forged out a will but didn't realize that Wagner never developed the ability to write in English.

"I hereby make my last will and testament," Anna wrote on behalf of Wagner. "I am of sound mind and no influence. I have my money in the Fifth Third Union bank. I want my funeral expenses paid and all my bills. The rest I leave to my relative, Anna Hahn of 2970 Colerain Avenue, who will be the executor of my estate. I want no flowers and I do not want to be laid out. (Signed) Jacob Wagner."

She would steal his money to pay off her gambling debts. But the addiction would not go away.

Anna simply could not stop herself from gambling.

She would go to the racetracks up to four times a week and her losses once again began to accrue.

"Anna was very smart when it came to selecting the right victim and circumstance," Orange said. "But she was too stupid to realize that she wasn't very good at picking a good horse. She had a compulsive personality disorder. Anything that she saw had a positive benefit would be repeated over and over again. She became good at getting into the graces of older men and taking their money. So that became another addiction that she had to feed."

MORE LONELY OLD MEN

Anna would meet another elderly man in the mostly German neighborhood. His name was George Heis. She would arrive at his home and entertain the old man with her charm and gaiety, making drinks for him as he sat on his couch.

"Mr. Heis was a coal dealer that she met and befriended," Franklin said. "She got very friendly with him. He would take the money he would collect from his coal deliveries and give it to her."

George lived it up with Anna, drinking up the best bourbon and laughing it up in his living room.

He didn't know that Anna was counting the days when she would kill him.

One night, she would lace his drink with arsenic. He would remain paralyzed for the rest of his life.

"Arsenic loves to attack the endothelial cells," Orange said. "Those that line the blood vessels. When it attacks, those blood vessels begin to leak. Leakage of blood anywhere, particularly in that central nervous system, can cause symptoms such as paralysis."

Heis drank Anna's poisonous concoction and immediately began gasping in pain. He stood up and staggered around the room.

Anna simply watched as the old man's eyes bugged out as he tried to make it to the bathroom.

"She was heartless," Orange said. "She would watch the old man stagger in front of her, begging for help. Her only response would be to take a sip from her own drink as he collapsed to the ground and writhed in pain."

Anna would not stop with George Heis. She continued to poison men and the community was none the wiser.

"Yeah, all these people were dying in this close-knit community," Franklin said. "And no one was saying a word. Eventually, someone spoke up and said 'Hey, we're missing one.' And they reported it to police. The police didn't believe it. They didn't have any evidence to go on and they would just slough it off."

The coal company began to inquire with Anna for the money she owed Heis. She had to find a new benefactor and found one in Albert Palmer, a retired railroad watchman who had a small pension. She would meet Palmer at the Blade, the gambling joint where Anna frequented. Palmer became smitten with the youthful Anna who wrote the lonely old man love notes, calling him, "my dear, sweet Dady" (sic) and would sign her notes to him "with all my love and kisses, your Ann."

"I wrote like that," Anna said," because I regarded him like a father."

Anna would borrow money from Palmer which she used to pay off the coal company. Anna had provided company to Palmer and cooked him "homestyle German meals." Palmer was smitten by Anna but not so smitten that he didn't want his money back. Anna then took care of the debt owed to the old man by giving him a nice helping of poison in his mashed potatoes.

Palmer then became ill and died on March 27th, 1937.

CATCH ME IF YOU CAN

Anna was getting away with murder with no end in sight.

"Even today, you don't suspect a woman of being a serial killer," Franklin said. "They're not that many. But maybe there are a lot more than we think because they're hard to detect. They're very hard to detect. Who would suspect a nice German lady like Anna Marie Hahn of being a serial killer? You just would not believe it and the police didn't either."

Anna was able to avoid detection because of her ability to think rationally and plan out her attacks. Unlike some of her fellow serial killers, her murders were not done on the spur of the moment. They were cold and calculating with Anna waiting for exactly the right time to execute her victim.

That next victim would be sixty-seven-year-old George Gsellman.

Lonely and pathetic, he nonetheless jumped at the chance to have the young German beauty as his caretaker. She waited on him hand and foot, cooking his meals and cleaning up around the house. Her son would also quickly befriend the sickly Gsellman whom she was slowly poisoning with arsenic and croton oil.

Anna would use the croton oil in order to flush the arsenic out of the system. The oil would cause almost immediate vomiting and on its own could cause death if the victim is not properly re-hydrated.

Anna would take Gsellman for all that the old man had. He would eventually die alone in his room.

"Anna's appetite to get what she wanted had no limits," Orange said. "She wanted that money. Needed that money. That being said, she probably enjoyed the rush of taking someone's life. You don't do something like that for so long without a psychological payoff of some kind. Anna kept killing men not only for profit but because she liked it."

THE DEATH OF JOHANN OBENDORFER

"2150 Clifton Avenue was the home of Johann Obendorfer," Franklin said. "On street level is his little cobble shop that Anna Marie walked into one day because she had broken her heel while out shopping. He fell in love with her but she had other designs. Can you imagine how happy he must have been to have snared this beautiful woman? Little did he know that in two weeks he would be dead."

Obendorfer was the typical lonely widow that Anna would target. She entertained his affection for her by telling him that they should go to Colorado and live on a ranch.

Obendorfer agreed. Accompanied by her son Oskar, Anna would travel with the elderly Obendorfer to Colorado.

But they never bought a ranch together.

Within one day of their arrival in Denver, Obendorfer became deathly ill in his hotel room after Anna gave him some food. He was taken to Bethel Hospital and Anna registered him as being from Chicago. "I didn't have any money," she said. "I didn't want to be responsible for any bill."

"By the time they got to Denver," Franklin said. "Mr. Obendorfer had gotten very, very sick. She had been poisoning him the whole trip."

She would deny knowing Obendorfer to the hospital staff. They inquired for some identification of the man and Anna leaned over her benefactor on his death bed.

"Old man," Anna said. "Tell these people your name. Tell them who you are."

Obendorfer could not even manage a whisper, he was so weak.

"I don't know who he is," Anna said, throwing her hands in the air. "He's just an old German that I met on the train."

Anna then left the hospital and felt that she wanted more out of the trip that what she was stealing from Oberdorfer. Prepping to leave town, she had one more heist in mind.

"The hotel owner had rooms right behind the registration desk," Franklin said. "One day Anna Marie walked right into one of those private rooms. She saw two diamond earrings on the dresser and stole them. When the hotel owner realized they were missing she filed a complaint with the police in Colorado Springs. By that time Anna Marie and her son had left town and left poor Mr. Obendorfer on a slab in the morgue."

An autopsy would reveal high levels of arsenic in Obendorfer's body.

While Anna was away in Colorado Springs, the police in Cincinnati had finally become suspicious of Anna. They searched her house and found some incriminating evidence.

The police would search through one of her purses and find a salt shaker with enough arsenic inside to kill off all the inhabitants of a small town. They also found a bottle of croton oil that was marked with the words "poison." They found a bottle which contained more than seventy grams of arsenic lodged between the rafters between the cellar and the first floor.

Upon returning home, Anna would be confronted by the police. They would interrogate her about the poison and Anna would deny ownership of the contents but want it back nonetheless.

The police chief at the time, a man named Hayes thought that his intimidating questions would force Anna to crack under pressure.

"There are an awful lot of men dying around you, Mrs. Hahn."

"I love to make old people comfy," Anna said. "It isn't my fault that all these old men are dying. I know it is very peculiar, but why pick on me, Chief?"

"We searched your place, Mrs. Hahn," Hayes said. "We found enough poison to kill half of Cincinnati."

"I have been like an angel of mercy to them. The last thing that would ever enter my head would be to harm those dear old men."

TIGHTENING THE NOOSE

Anna would visit a physician named Dr. Vos whose office was in a building Annie owned and occupied. The doctor would soon discover that many of his blank prescription forms were missing. Anna's husband Philip would come forward with a bottle of poison and inform police that Anna had, in fact, stolen the prescription forms. She would forge the doctor's signature and order the poisons from the local pharmacist.

"She would send our twelve-year-old son, Oskar, to get the prescriptions. One pharmacist refused to fill the prescription because of the boy's age."

Philip then told police that Anna had tried twice to insure his life for $25,000 but he had refused to sign off. After his refusal, Philip began to become ill with the same symptoms as some of Anna's previous victims.

Philip's mother demanded that she take her son to the hospital where it was revealed that he was being poisoned. He recovered but never spoke to his wife again.

With the evidence provided by Philip the police now had enough to arrest Anna Marie Hahn.

On August 10th, 1937, Anna would be placed behind bars.

"She got too cocky," Orange said. "She would leave behind too many clues, in particular with Obendorfer. She forgot to cover her trail and the police eventually got her on their radar. The irony was that the predator, Anna, now became the prey of the police as they spent months gathering evidence on her."

Anna would plead not guilty to the charges of murdering Gsellman. She claimed that she didn't know the man. But a friend of Gsellman told the police that they had witnessed Anna visiting the old man the night before he died.

The investigation grew in scope as the deaths of five other old men and another couple had all died without warning but with one thing in common.

They all were friends of Anna Marie.

THE TRIAL AND EXECUTION

"It took me a long, long time to find that it is wrong to be good to people," Anna said to a reporter outside her trial. "This doesn't mean I am going to be hateful from now on because that is against my nature. They can take a human's body, but they can't take their soul because that will go where there is justice."

When her case went to trial, it shocked a nation that had never seen a female serial killer before.

During the trial, newspaper reporters described Anna as "poker-faced, blonde German woman who at no time displayed any appearance of resentment or shock at anything that has been said."

The prosecutor in the case spared Anna no mercy.

"In the four corners of this courtroom are four dead men," he bellowed. "These men are pointing their bony fingers at this woman as they say, 'That woman poisoned me. She made me die in agony. She made me suffer the tortures of the damned. Let my death not be in vain."

The defense attorney argued back that the evidence against Anna was circumstantial and that she was a "victim of a cruel sequence of coincidence."

"What was shocking to everyone," Franklin said. "Was that the jury returned a verdict of guilty without mercy."

The jury would be comprised of eleven women and one man. The prosecuting attorney felt that if the jury was comprised of a male majority they would see Anna as a sympathetic figure. So they stacked it in favor of females.

The guilty verdict meant that Anna would be the first woman in Ohio history to be sentenced to death in the electric chair.

Anna still had enough charm and wit to play on the sympathy of people.

"The judge cried," Franklin said. "Because he had to sentence Anna Marie to death. He had no choice."

"At the end of the day, Anna proved to be like most every other serial killer," Orange said. "She thought that everyone else was beneath her in terms of intelligence. They don't think they can be caught and the vastly underestimate the scope and IQ level of the people around them which include the police. Anna thought she was more cunning that everyone around her. For awhile, she was. Then the noose tightened around her neck and she had nowhere to go."

The night before her execution, Anna would sit down and write out a twenty-page confession of all of her murders. She tearfully described every detail in the small journal, addressing it to "Dear Lord."

"On one hand, you can look at her confessional as a letter begging for forgiveness," Orange said. "But women like Anna aren't remorseful without a payoff. Cold and heartless, she wanted to remain in control until her final breath. Her confessional letter was yet another attempt at control. She wanted to be in charge until the very end."

"I do not show my feelings," Anna wrote. "My troubles in life, starting when I had my baby, had taught me how to control my feelings...I don't know what made me do it. All that I can say is that my troubles were so big that it must have turned my mind. I do not try to excuse myself or my actions. They were not me at all...It all seems like a horrible dream...I wanted to cry out that they were trying the other Anna Hahn and not this one sitting in the courtroom...Maybe it would have been different if I had only told my lawyers the truth. My lawyers fought so hard for me. But that is all over now...I do not fear my end and my last concern is only for my boy. I have written this confession with the full knowledge that death is near and I only ask one favor and that is that my son should not be judged for the wrongs that his mother may have done."

The sale of Anna's confession to the newspapers allowed Anna's attorneys to take care of Oskar's future. They moved him away from Cincinnati and had him placed under a new name. Her husband Philip would remarry shortly after the trial.

There are competing reports of how Anna behaved as she waited to be executed. Some reports describe her as pleading to see her son for one last time. Others describe her as mocking that report, sarcastically asking "do I look like someone who is distraught?"

Nonetheless, before being executed Anna pleaded for mercy. She had reached out to Ohio Governor Daley to grant a stay of execution.

"This was one of the most difficult decisions I've ever had to make," Governor Davey said. "Something inside me sort of rebelled against the idea of allowing a woman to go to the chair but the crimes committed by Hahn were so cold-blooded, so deliberately planned and executed that I have no choice but to permit the decision of the court to stand. I feel sorry for her son, Oscar, but his mother has bequeathed him nothing to be proud of."

Anna would be sent to the electric chair on December 7th, 1938 at the Ohio Penitentiary in Colombus, Ohio. She refused to see her husband and son on the last night of her life but allowed reporters covering her trial a farewell party. Several of the newsmen entered Anna's cell. She had fruit punch and cake prepared for them.

"You gave me a 'good show' at my trial, boys," Anna said. "The least I could do was to throw a bash for you. I guess I'm not much like a 'beautiful blonde' now, huh? Well, give me a good write-up when it's all over."

THE ELECTRIC CHAIR

"Don't do this to me!" Anna screamed at the prison attendants who began strapping the electric belts to her leg. She writhed against the grip of the guards as they held her down, strapping her to the chair.

Anna screamed in mercy. A priest entered the room just as the black death mask was placed over her head. Her screams and pleas became inaudible.

"Our Father, who are in heaven," the priest said.

Anna could be heard repeating the prayer until the execution flipped the switched as the heavy jolts of electricity crackled through her body.

She screamed for mercy then continued the Lord's Prayer.

"But deliver us-"

Those were her final words.

It took two and a half minutes to kill Anna Marie Hahn on the electric chair.

"Did she protest her innocence to the last?" a news reporter asked her attorney, Joseph Hoodin.

"I won't comment on that," Hoodin said.

"But did she admit her guilt?"

"I understood the question," Hoodin said. "And I still won't comment."

Anna would be buried at the Mount Calvary Cemetery in Cincinnati, Ohio.

HUSBAND KILLER : THE TRUE STORY OF AUDREY MARIE HILLEY

ANNA DELANEY

Audrey Marie Hilley

"That woman was pitiful," said Janice Hinds, 50, one of two neighbours who called police and cared for Hilley after spotting her sprawled on the deck of Thomason's home.

"We didn't know she was Marie Hilley. She didn't look like Marie Hilley," said Hinds, who grew up in the same Blue Mountain cotton-mill town as Hilley. "Marie Hilley was a sophisticated lady. She had pride in her looks, her dress."[1]

Her Early Life

Audrey Marie Hilley was born on June 4th, 1933 in Blue Mountain, Alabama. Her parents, Huey and Lucille Frazier, worked hard at the Linen Mill to provide for their family, and Marie (as she was known) was often looked after by relatives when her mother returned to work shortly after she was born.

Huey and Lucille loved their only child but showed their love with material things rather than affection and time. She was always well-dressed and had nice things, and as a result, Marie became rather spoilt. She was well known for her temper tantrums when things didn't go her way, and her parents, possibly out of guilt for not being there, rarely checked her for her behaviour.[2]

The Fraziers were proud people and were determined that their only child would not spend her life working in the same mills as they, and most of the town's inhabitants, had always done. They wanted more for their daughter and instilled in her an ambition to be a secretary, a lofty ambition for someone from a mill town.

In 1945, the Fraziers moved from Blue Mountain to Anniston, and Marie enrolled at Quintard Junior High School. Anniston was a whole new world to the girl who had felt she was above the rest in her old hometown. Marie went from being a big fish in a small pond to a small fish in a much more upscale lake, and for the first time in her life found herself at a disadvantage. In Anniston, all the girls wore nice dresses and what was more, some of their parents were the owners of the same mills that Marie's parents worked at.

Marie threw herself into her studies, making a name for herself as a diligent, intelligent student, and she integrated herself into new social circles – her friends were from privileged families and Marie wanted to be a part of that.

It wasn't just the teachers for whom Marie stood out, though. She was also a pretty girl and had her fair share of the attention from the boys, too. In fact, by the end of the 7th grade of Junior High School, Marie Hilley had been voted the prettiest girl in school by the yearbook staff.

It was around this time that 16-year-old Frank Hilley noticed 12-year-old Marie, and by the time he graduated High School, he was in love.[3]

Frank and Marie

In contrast to the Frazier family, who loved their daughter but showed no affection, Frank Hilley's family was warm and affectionate. The Hilleys worked in the other big industry of the area – pipe making - and even though they did not have much money, Clarence and Carrie Hilley made a happy, comfortable home for their three children – Frank, Jewel and Freeda.

Marie's parents did not approve of Frank – he was not from one of the affluent families of Anniston and Huey and Lucille wanted more for their daughter – but Marie was happy to be Frank's girl, and in return, he treated her like a princess.

Frank joined the Navy after finishing High School and was assigned to Guam but the distance between them bothered Frank. He was worried that with him so far away, and with so much time apart, Marie might find someone else so, on May 8th, 1951, before 17-year-old Marie had even finished High School, the young couple married.

Married Life

Marie remained in Anniston to finish her education and then joined Frank in Long Beach, California before the couple moved to Boston where Frank finished his stint in the Navy. It was while they were in Boston that they discovered Marie was pregnant with their first child, and the couple moved back to Anniston and bought a small home. Frank secured a job with a local foundry, and Marie found work as a secretary. Like all couples, the pair had their ups and downs, but for the most part, they seemed happy.

Their first child, Michael Hilley, was born on November 11th, 1952.

The Troubles Begin

Marie had been brought up to want the best of everything. While Frank was still in the Navy he had sent all of his paychecks home to his young wife, and yet when the time had come for her to join her new husband in California she had no money to pay for the journey. She had been spending his wages without telling him, and his parents had had to finance Marie's travel in order for her to join her new husband.

Despite the extra financial burdens having a young baby places on a family, Marie's spending didn't decrease. She wanted nice clothes and expensive home furnishings, and Frank, not liking to upset his wife, gave in to her, just as her parents had when she was a girl. Marie was a woman who was used to getting her own way.[4]

In 1959 Marie's behaviour began to become more sinister. She started taunting Frank, waving love letters she said were from other men in front of him but not letting him read them. She would then leave the torn up pieces where her husband could find them. Frank pieced them together, and it became clear that his wife had written them herself. When he confronted her she said she was afraid he didn't love her anymore and wanted to make him jealous.

By this time, Marie was spending double her take-home pay from her own job on fine clothes and luxuries. To prevent Frank, who was extremely responsible financially, from finding out she would get up early in the morning to check the mail and hide the bills.

Marie became pregnant again, and on January 14th, 1960 she gave birth to a baby daughter, whom they named Carol Marie.[5]

Carol

By the time Carol was born, things should have been looking up for the family. Frank had been promoted at work, and Marie had developed a reputation as a first class executive secretary. However, as the family's income rose, so did Marie's spending. Furthermore, she was becoming known for a peculiar situation at work. While her bosses loved her for her politeness and diligence, her co-workers greatly disliked her. They found her to be very judgemental of those around her and felt that she put on airs and graces and acted as if her co-workers were 'beneath' her. When she became disliked she would leave, and complain to friends and family that her colleagues had 'ganged up' on her and driven her from her job. Her employers, though, always gave her exemplary references, and she never found it difficult to get another job. In fact, Marie Hilley worked for some of the most powerful and affluent men in Anniston.[6]

Marie was disappointed with her daughter, Carol. She wanted her daughter to wear pretty dresses and have bows in her hair, while Carol was more of a tomboy and would often go to football games with her father. The pair developed a close father/daughter relationship and Marie was deeply resentful and jealous. She lamented the fact that her daughter was not feminine and demure and the pair argued constantly. Marie was much closer to her son, Mike, and like her parents before her never dished out discipline. Materially, the children wanted for nothing. Emotionally, it was a different story.

Going Up in the World

In 1962, Marie instigated a move to McClellan Boulevard, which was much closer to the houses of the affluent residents of Anniston that she so desperately tried to emulate. She felt that they were 'her' people. That same year, Marie's parents – Huey and Lucille moved in with the Hilleys.[7]

Marie's behaviour was becoming more and more out of control, and Frank was becoming increasingly concerned. He would often sit up with her during the night as she shook violently, unable to calm her. Perhaps the financial hole she had dug for the family was beginning to take its toll on Marie's psyche – by this time she had opened a Post Office Box and was having some of her bills sent there in order to avoid detection by Frank.

When the money ran out Marie started taking out loans. Frank was a well-respected man in the area and loans were secured against his good name and standing in the community. But creditors became concerned when bills and loan payment dates came and went without being settled, as Frank had always been a man who paid on time.[8]

On December 11th, 1965, Marie's father, Huey, died of cancer at the age of 57.[9]

In 1972, Mike graduated from High School and decided to pursue a career in the ministry, for which he went away to college.

Marie's behaviour towards her daughter, Carol, became more extreme. She often accused her of being a lesbian and would rant at Carol's female friends. Her paranoia at being found out in the lies regarding money must have been affecting her, because she also, around this time, stopped Frank from talking to his friends on the 'phone. It was also around this period of time that Frank Hilley became sick.[[10]

Frank

During 1974 Frank had long periods of sickness. He put his frequent illnesses down to something he'd eaten, but soon the fatigue, vomiting and nausea could not be explained away by food. One day Frank came home from work early after succumbing to yet another bout of sickness, to find his wife in bed with her boss. His wife's spending suddenly made sense – she was sleeping with her employers for money. Frank was disgusted with his wife's behaviour but felt too ill and weak to deal with it. Instead, he turned to his son, Mike, who was by this time an ordained minister.[11]

However, that phone call, in which Frank arranged to meet Mike in Georgia where he now lived, was overheard by Audrey, who was listening in on an extension. From that moment on, Frank's symptoms worsened considerably, and he became seriously ill.[12]

On May 19th, 1975 Frank couldn't stand it any longer, and he consulted Dr Earl Jones, who diagnosed him initially with a viral stomach ache.[13] Dr Earl prescribed various medications, but nothing seemed to be helping. Frank's sister Freeda came to visit him, and he told her that he feared he was going to die, as he had never been so sick. He also told her that Marie had been administering him medicine via a syringe on the Dr's orders.[14]

On May 23rd, 1975, Frank was admitted to the Regional Medical Center. Tests indicated liver failure, and subsequently infectious hepatitis.[15] Frank was desperately ill, jaundiced and hallucinating. Mike, who had travelled to be with his father, had to restrain Frank from jumping out of the window. In the early hours of May 25th, Mike left the hospital to pick up his Grandmothers so that they could see Frank, but when he returned his mother was asleep and his father was dead. Frank Hilley was 45.[16]

Because of Frank's sudden death, an autopsy was performed, with Marie's blessing. Tests showed that Frank did indeed have hepatitis, along with swelling of the lungs and kidneys, inflammation of the stomach, and bilateral pneumonia.[17]

Life After Frank

With Frank's death being confirmed as being of natural causes, Marie made a claim on his life insurance and received a payment of $31,140.[18] Marie went on a spending spree, indulging her love of luxury items. She bought new clothes, jewelery, and a new car. Her mother, Lucille, was still living with Marie and Carol and received a diamond ring. Carol herself was treated to numerous gifts, including a car and a stereo. It was hardly the behaviour of a grieving widow.[19]

In 1976 Mike and his then wife Teri moved in with the family. Shortly after Frank's death, Lucille had been diagnosed with cancer. Her health was failing and they were happy to help. However, it wasn't a good move for the young couple. Marie was restless, and often complained to anyone who would listen that nobody loved her, and would frequently complain about her boss and her job. She was highly dissatisfied with her life, and to make matters worse Marie and Carol fought endlessly, making family life fraught. Mike would often find himself torn between his mother, who would constantly demand his attention, and his wife, Teri, who had begun experiencing ill health since moving in with Marie. Hospitalised four times with illness, Teri also suffered a miscarriage, and the young couple decided to move out.

They found an apartment and were ready to move in, but the night before their move Marie's house caught fire. Mike and Teri moved into their apartment, with Marie, Carol and Lucille in tow. Repairs were soon made to Marie's house, but the night before his mother was due to go home, Mike's neighbour's apartment suffered the same fate and went up in flames. Mike and Teri had no choice but to move back in with Marie, Carol and Lucille. They were back where they began.[20]

A Strange Series of Events

Mike and Teri finally found their own home and moved away from Marie. On January 4^(th), 1977, Lucille lost her battle against widespread, aggressive cancer. Marie again came into money – a small sum of $600 from a burial policy.

Marie became well known to the local police. She was constantly reporting strange occurrences at her home. As well as petty thefts, she claimed that a fire had been started in her closet late one night. Coincidentally, Marie's neighbour, Doris Ford reported an almost identical fire in her own house (to which Marie had a key) the same night. There followed a succession of reports by both women of nuisance phone calls and other grievances.

Marie came up with many theories about where the harassment of both herself and her neighbour was coming from. She told Detective Gary Caroll that she suspected someone at the phone company of making the calls, as the calls seemed only to happen when the trace was taken off of her phone. She also claimed that one of her former employers had tried to force her to have sex and was harassing her because of her refusal. Yet another theory put forward by Marie was that, shortly after Frank's death, two men had arrived at her house demanding repayment of gambling debts.

When police put a trace on Doris Ford's phone, however, the calls were traced back to the Jenkins Manufacturing Plant, which just so happened to be where Marie was working.[21]

In 1978, Marie and Carol moved to Florida to live with Mike and Teri. Carol had just graduated, and Marie found herself a job in an office. Her out of control spending habits continued to cause problems when she ran up over $600 on Mike's credit card, promising to pay him back. This living arrangement only lasted a few short months, however, before Marie and Carol returned to Anniston.[22]

Mike and Teri were happy to see Marie leave. By that time they had a baby son called Joshua, and Mike feared that Marie would take the baby and disappear as she seemed to have an unhealthy fixation on him.[23]

Carol's Turn

Marie had no home of her own to return to when she and Carol moved back to Anniston. At first, they stayed with Freeda, Frank's sister, and then they moved in with Carrie Hilley, Frank's mother. Once they were settled at Carrie's house, the strange happenings recommenced. Items went missing, phone lines were cut, and small fires were started. Illness also struck the household – Carrie Hilley started suffering from nausea and vomiting.

Marie started a new job, and very quickly started an affair with her boss, Harold Dillard, and began manipulating him to leave his wife. At the same time, she also started seeing Calvin Robertson, an old school friend. Calvin believed Marie when she told him she had cancer and needed expensive treatment, and he gladly gave her the money for the 'fictitious' illness. When Marie told him some time later that she was now cancer-free he was elated, and so smitten that he would have done anything for her.

It was also during this time that Marie began buying insurance policies. Not only did she take out fire insurance, cancer insurance, and her own life insurance, she also took out insurance policies on the lives of her two children. Mike was insured for $25,000 while Carol had two policies on her life, totalling $39,000.

Carol's senior prom came in April 1979. During the evening Carol started to feel ill. It wasn't enough to make her leave the party, though, so she ignored her symptoms. The next day, however, she was so ill during a church service that she had to leave the service early and vomited in the car park. Coincidentally, Carrie Hilley had also taken ill at church and was taken to hospital after fainting.[24]

By August 1979 Carol had been admitted to the Emergency Room several times with nausea and vomiting. After yet another episode of sickness in August, Marie gave her daughter an injection into her hip, which she said would ease the nausea. Instead of easing, however, Carol's illness took a serious downturn. Not only did the injection not ease Carol's sickness, it also caused her fingers and legs to become numb and weak.

On August 22nd, 1979 she was admitted to the Anniston Hospital by Dr Warren Sarrell. When, by August 29th Dr Sarrell had been unable to find a cause for Carol's symptoms, he sent her for a psychiatric evaluation at the Carraway Methodist Hospital in Birmingham. While under the care of Dr John Elmore, Carol was given two further injections by her mother – injections which, she was told, would help with her weak legs. She told Carol that the injections had been supplied by Doris Ford, who was a registered nurse, and that Carol could tell no-one as Doris would get into trouble if she was found out.

On September 18th, 1979, with Carol still in the hospital, Marie asked Dr Elmore what was wrong with her daughter. He told her that she was suffering from vitamin deficiencies and malnutrition, and, in his opinion, lead poisoning. Carol took exception to this diagnosis and, against Dr Elmore's advice, discharged Carol from the hospital.

On September 19th, Carol was once again admitted to the hospital, this time to the University of Alabama Hospital in Birmingham. The same day, Marie was arrested as her fraudulent ways finally caught up with her. Her arrest was what, ultimately, saved Carol's life. Marie was taken in for questioning, and Carol was examined by Dr Brian Thompson, who noticed that, along with the numbness in her hands and feet, Carol also had striations on her nails, called Aldridge Mee's Lines. He explained that these markings were typical of arsenic poisoning, and ordered tests on Carol's hair.

The initial findings revealed that Carol had over 50 times the normal arsenic level of human hair. Shockingly, when more detailed tests were carried out on October 3rd, 1979 they showed that the hair close to Carol's scalp had over 100 times the normal levels, while hair further down the hair shaft the levels were lower, right down to zero at the ends. This indicated, according to Forensic Scientist John Case, that Carol had been systematically poisoned with arsenic over a period of four to eight months, with the dosages given in increasingly higher strengths.

Furthermore, with Marie unable to be with her daughter, Carol's conditioned improved dramatically during her time at the hospital.[25]

On the strength of these findings, Frank Hilley's body was exhumed, and once again large levels of arsenic were found. His cause of death was changed to that of arsenic poisoning. The same substance was also discovered to have been present in both Lucille Frazier and Carrie Hilley (who had died recently) at the time of their deaths, although not fatal amounts.[26]

On October 9th, 1979, while still incarcerated for the fraudulent charges, Marie Hilley was arrested for the attempted murder of Carol. As part of their ongoing, and increasingly serious, investigations the Anniston police found a vial in Marie's purse – a vial which testing confirmed contained arsenic.

On November 9th, 1979, Marie made bail and was released, under the name of Emily Stephens, to a local motel. However, Marie was not going to just sit and await her trial, and somewhere between October 9th and October 18th, Marie disappeared. A note was found in her motel room, suggesting that she 'might' have been kidnapped.

Audrey Marie Hilley was now a fugitive and would remain so for more than three years.[27]

A New Identity

There were only a few clues for the police to go on after Marie disappeared. Margaret Key, Marie's Aunt, reported that her home had been broken into and that her car and some clothes had disappeared. The police called in the FBI, but once the car was found abandoned in Georgia the trail went cold very quickly.

On January 11th, 1980, Marie Hilley, still a fugitive, was indicted for the murder of her husband, Frank Hilley.

Marie, meanwhile, had assumed a new identity in Florida. Robbi Hannon, as she was now known, was working her charm on a man called John Homan. Robbi told John tales of her imaginary tragic past, and John, who hadn't had the easiest of lives himself, fell for both the stories and for Robbi. She told him that she had lost her children in a car accident and John felt as though he had found a kindred spirit.

He fell in love, hook, line, and sinker.

On May 29th, 1981 Robbi and John were married, after which they moved to Marlow, New Hampshire. They both found work there and rented a house. Robbi's new job was in customer service at the Central Screw Corporation, where she excelled. The men found her to be fun, while her co-workers, for the most part, found her pleasant, although a few took a dislike to her. She regaled the staff with stories of a wealthy family in Texas, whose fortune she would inherit one day, and garnered sympathy by telling them about her two children dying in a car accident.

She would also talk of an identical twin sister called Teri Martin, who lived in Texas, making frequent reference to her.

Robbi would, from time to time, complain of searing headaches, and told John that she was seeking treatment from specialists. Until one day, Robbi came to John and told him it had been discovered that she was suffering from an incurable blood disease. It was her twin sister, Teri, who would be looking after Robbi when she made one last trip to Texas in search of a cure, and in September 1982, Robbi left Marlow to seek treatment.

Of course, there was no incurable disease, and no twin sister, either. Robbi only stayed in Texas for a few days, and then made her way to Florida, where she bleached her hair blond, and found work as a secretary, using the name Teri Martin. During her six weeks at her new job, Teri confided in her boss, Jack McKenzie, about her terminally ill twin sister Robbie. In early November, Teri called Jack and told him Robbi had died, and that she was needed in New Hampshire.

On November 10th, 'Teri' called John Homan and told him his wife had died, and the following day she flew back to New Hampshire.

During her time away, 'Teri' had lost a lot of weight, and changed her hair color to blond, so John easily accepted that this was his dead wife's twin sister. The pair went to the local paper and placed an obituary for Robbi, and then John took Teri to his wife's workplace – The Central Screw Corporation – and introduced the workers to Robbi's twin sister. While some of the staff accepted Teri's appearance, some did not and were highly suspicious.

Teri insisted on moving in with John Homan, saying they needed to help each other grieve, and she found herself a job as a secretary at a book printing company.

Meanwhile, the suspicions were still rising at Robbi's old workplace, and a few of the doubters decided to take a closer look into Robbi's obituary. Their suspicions were confirmed when they discovered that the details mentioned in the paper were fictitious, and they took those suspicions to the police.

Arrested

On January 12th, 1983, the police apprehended Teri at work. They had been watching her and thought she might be another fugitive, Terry Lynn Clifton. However, when they asked her her name she told them it was Audrey Marie Hilley, and that she was wanted for fraud. The local police ran a check on her name and discovered that she was wanted for much more than bad checks.

On January 19th, 1983, Marie was brought back to Anniston. Carol was desperate to see her mother, to find some answers, but although Marie professed her love for her daughter she gave no explanation for the poisoning. Prosecutors were worried that Carol's love for her mother would go in Marie's favour and that Carol would not say anything against her mother.

They needn't have worried.

Carol's testimony about her mother giving her the injections was solid. Marie had told her attorneys that after her arrest in 1979 she had been interviewed but she failed to mention that that interview had been recorded. During that interview, Marie admitted to giving Carol the injections and the recording was there for all to hear. Carol's defense fell apart.

The jury needed only three hours to return their verdicts – guilty of the murder of Frank Hilley, and of the attempted murder of Carol Hilley.

Judge Sam Monk sentenced Marie to life imprisonment for Frank's murder, plus twenty years for the poisonings, and on June 9th, 1983, Marie was taken to Tutwiler State Women's Prison in Wetumpka, Alabama.

Marie's Escape

Marie was a perfect prisoner. She never caused trouble and was classified as a minimum security prisoner. This classification meant that she was eligible for leave from the prison. Between late 1986 and February 1987, Marie had left prison for eight hours on four occasions, returning on time with each leave.

On February 19th, 1987, Marie left the prison on a three-day leave pass. John had, by this time, moved to Anniston so that he and his wife could spend her leave together whenever they could.

On February 22nd, Marie arranged to meet John at her parents' graves. Marie never showed up, and John found, instead, a note from his wife.

"I hope you will be able to forgive me," it read. *"I'm getting ready to leave. It will be best for everybody. We'll be together again. Please give me an hour to get out of town."*

John took the note to the police, and, given Marie's past cunning, they assumed she was already far out of state, and started, once again, searching for her.[28]

Her Death

Marie hadn't gone far. On February 26th, 1987, Aniston police received a phone call. Marie had been found huddled behind a house, apparently having wandered in the woods for four days. The weather had been terrible – heavy rain and low temperatures – and Marie was suffering from hypothermia and delirium. Marie started having convulsions, and, in the ambulance on the way to the hospital, Audrey Marie Hilley took her last breath.

On February 28th, 1987, Marie was buried next to her husband, Frank, at their children's request.[29] Her second husband, John Homan, died two years later in 1989 while working as a caretaker in Anniston. He intervened in a fight and was stabbed to death. Marie's note to John, in which she said that they would be together again, had come true a lot sooner than anyone would have predicted.[30]

HOUSEWIFE, MOTHER & KILLER : THE TRUE STORY OF KIM HRICKO

82

DARLA PUGH

PROLOGUE

Kim Hricko was getting ready to kill her husband the night they attended a Valentine's Murder Mystery Party. Kim was a woman who was intelligent and determined, the irony of the play's theme was not lost on her.

It was destiny calling.

She watched with rapt attention as the actors went through the motions. A wedding bride took out a blue vial and poured the "poisonous" contents into her groom's champagne glass.

She has the right idea, Kim thought.

Looking over at her husband Steve, she imagined him in the place of the actor on stage, choking to death.

Could it be that easy?

CHAPTER ONE

"Kim Hricko was one of those people that you look at and say 'I would never have guessed,'" forensic psychologist Paula Orange said. "Something inside her snapped when she wanted out of her marriage. It could have been so simple. Call a lawyer and file for divorce. Kim wanted a lot more than that. She wanted blood."

Steve and Kim Hricko would be introduced by their mutual friends Maureen and Mike Miller at Penn State in 1984. Their temperaments seemed to be the perfect complement to one another, they would have a yin-yang compatibility.

"Kim was a very gregarious personality," Maureen said. "She was very outgoing. Very friendly. Everybody liked her."

"Steve was my best friend since seventh grade," Mike said. "Corny as it sounds we were kinda each others brother that we didn't have. My wife had set up a double date. He (Steve) was smitten by her. Thought she was very attractive. Basically, they hit it off and from that point on started dating."

Steve was a burly figure at 6'3" and 245 lbs. He was a star college football player but was on the shy side.

"He was a big teddy bear," Maureen said. "He just wanted everybody that he loved to be happy and for him to take care of them."

Neither Kim or Steve dated much before their union. Kim had a distant relationship with her father after her own parents divorced. Her mother would remarry a man that would sexually and physically abuse her.

Steve and Kim would marry and have a daughter. Nine years into their marriage, Steve would still be smitten by the woman that the Millers had set him up with. Kim, however, would have feelings of resentment that built up over time.

Temperamentally, the couple did not match up well. Steve was an introvert. Kim an extrovert. Kim hung out with doctors and nurses while Steve just wanted to stay home. He didn't feel welcome into Kim's elite social circle, put off by their large houses and flashy cars.

But Steve remained in love with Kim despite that over the years she did not treat him with the same warmth as she once did. She was now cold and disinterested toward her spouse.

Steve blamed himself for the deterioration and began working to save his marriage.

His efforts would only serve to pour fuel on the fire...

CHAPTER TWO

Kim fed up with the loveless relationship, suggested that they get a divorce but Steve refused. He also dismissed the idea of counseling but after nine years he finally saw it as a last resort.

Steve went to counseling on his own and began taking steps to show Kim how much he truly cared. One of the first things he did was write his wife a long, heartfelt love letter.

Kim shared the letter with some of her friends who remarked at how beautiful it was. But Steve's words of love and devotion had no effect on Kim.

"Can you believe this shit?" Kim mocked as she read some passages aloud. "I am willing to do whatever it takes to save our marriage. It takes two of us. But I know we can do it. Together."

"I think that's sweet," her friend remarked.

"Gag me," Kim rolled her eyes. "Trust me, when you've been married as long as I have this kind of syrupy shit only makes you sick."

"I wish my husband would write me love letters."

"No," Kim said. "You don't. They keep coming and they don't stop. He's smothering me and following me around the house like a puppy dog."

Steve's renewed efforts to rekindle a long dead marriage were now being met with resentment. He was earnest in displaying his affection and becoming more communicative with Kim.

"Let's talk about our feelings," he said to his wife who stiffened with his every touch.

Kim would go to work eager to vent. She would open up about her marital difficulties to anyone who was willing to listen. She found a confidante in Jennifer Gowen.

"He is suffocating me," Kim told Gowen. "Stifling me. Following me around the damn house the whole time and cuddling with me at night. I can't even breathe. He's always asking me where I'm going or what I'm doing. Now he's calling me on my cell just to say 'Hi'. He never used to do that. It is annoying as shit."

But Steve was merely following the advise of his counsel. He had not dated much before Kim and she was his first serious relationship. He had no idea what to do when the relationship turned sour.

"It has to be said that Steve was on the receiving end of some very bad counseling advice," Orange said. "Appeasement never works and that is something that any decent psychiatrist or counselor should know. He kept turning the other cheek with Kim and that just fueled her resentment of him even more. This isn't to justify his murder, of course."

With his counseling session inspired efforts not yielding any results, Steve became distraught. He had done everything by the book but it wasn't working. He called his close friend Mike and opened up about his marriage and job difficulties.

"I don't know what to do, man," Steve said, his voice quaking with emotion. "I don't want to lose her. She's my life. My family is my everything. I feel like I've already lost her."

"Take it easy," Mike said. "We'll figure something out."

"What do you think I should do?" Steve asked.

"You need to take her out," Mike said "Someplace special. You know. Make a memory."

"Yeah," Steve said. "I know that. But I'm at a loss at how to go about it. I've tried everything."

"Tell you what," Mike said. "You come over to the Golf Resort."

"Harbourtowne?"

"I'll make sure you get the honeymoon cottage we have here. The very best one."

"You're too cool, Mike."

"Anytime, brother."

Mike worked at the Harbourtowne Golf Resort and set up the accommodations for his good friend and his wife. The place was hosting a Valentine's Day Murder Mystery play. Mike knew that the place worked wonders for romance. If there was anyplace that could rekindle the spark in a relationship, the resort would be it.

But Steve didn't know that Kim already had a romance of her own. His name was Brad Winkler.

CHAPTER THREE

Kim had met Brad Winkler when she was planning out the bachelorette party for her co-worker, Jennifer Gowen. Jennifer had brought Brad to the wedding shower ahead of time and the United States Marine was the only man at the party aside from Steve.

Kim and the young man hit it off immediately. She gave him a ride home along with Norma Walz after the party was over. They dropped off Brad at his aunt's house and Kim watched from the car as the young man made his way inside.

"He was in a bad marriage," Kim said to Norma. "Pretty sad. He's a nice guy. Jesus. The girl who catches him is going to be a lucky one. He's really sweet."

Kim returned home and was chastised by Steve for spending so much time with Brad. He had no idea of the affair to come.

Jennifer Gowen would get married and enlist the aid of Brad to help around the house while she was away on her honeymoon. Jennifer had a one-year-old daughter and Brad would babysit the girl and do some chores around the place.

Kim would come over and help out with the baby on the day Gowen left.

The affair with Brad would begin that night. They would have their trysts at Jen's townhouse while his cousin was still on her honeymoon. When Jennifer returned, the couple would continue their affair at the home of Brad's aunt.

Kim was equally open about her affair with Brad Winkler among friends as she was about her dissatisfaction with her marriage.

"I'm seeing someone," Kim said to Rachel, her college friend.

"You're having an affair?"

"Its just sex," Kim said, shrugging her shoulder. "I'm not going to marry this guy."

Kim kept up the charade on the home front as she plotted her next move. The change in her behavior made Steve believe that his efforts were working as he chronicled in his journal.

"Life at home is improving," Steve wrote. "I am looking forward to Valentine's weekend at Harbourtowne with Kim. She called twice today and said 'I love you' without me saying it first. I was very happy. Kim and I have not made love yet and I want to but I will wait as long as it takes. I love her...I believe I know what being in love really is. We have been married nine years but I feel like we just started dating."

Sadly, four days after Steve wrote those words in his journal Kim was off buying Brad Winkler a Valentine's Day gift.

"Brad, I really want to give you all these gifts in person but I guess the Pentagon had a different idea," Kim wrote. "I am so proud of what you do so I'll just go on missing you. Have a nice weekend at home, baby. I look forward to seeing you soon. Happy Valentine's Day, sir. I love you so very much. Hugs and Kisses, Kim."

While Steve had an optimistic view of their future life together, Kim continued to tell anyone with a listening ear about her dissatisfaction.

"There is a lot of verbal abuse," Kim said to Theresa Armstrong, one of her neighbors. "From both of us. He doesn't do anything. I do everything. I am unhappy and don't want to be married to him anymore."

She then went to her job at Holy Cross Hospital and told her co-worker Norma Walz about her problems.

"I've been in a bad marriage for a long time," Kim said. "Me and Steve have been having problems for a long time. A very long time."

"I always suspected that something wasn't right," Norma said.

"I've been living a lie," Kim nodded. I wanted him to go to counseling two years ago. Now he's going. And he's driving me crazy."

Steve's constant fawning and pandering annoyed Kim so much that she began thinking about what life would be like without him.

"You know if my husband dies we'd be better off than if we got a divorce," Kim told one of her neighbors. "Steve doesn't make that much money. He's a groundskeeper. We get a divorce and I'm paying him alimony. But if he died, well, if he died we would inherit $450,000 from his life insurance."

"That's a morbid thing to think about," the neighbor said, trying to laugh it off.

"You read about these stories all the time. The husband killing off the wife and vice-versa. I always wondered why they did it instead of just getting a divorce. It's the life insurance. Just like in the movies."

"What was lost in Kim's rationalizing was the fact that the killers most always get caught," Orange said. "But in her mind, she was the special one. Narcissists always think like that. Like they are the special one that won't get caught. Still, Kim needed that reassurance from her peers that she was doing the right thing as crazy as it sounds."

After not getting a receptive response from her neighbor, Kim once again turned to Jennifer Gowen.

"Steve would be better off dead," Kim said, using the same line on Jennifer. "We talked about getting a divorce but Steve doesn't want that. Even if he did he is going to try and turn Anna against me or try to keep her. He doesn't have a life outside our marriage so he is better off dead anyway."

"You really shouldn't talk like that. Let alone think like that."

"Why not? I thought about telling him about Brad but I think he would just get depressed or suicidal. Then I would not be able to collect the insurance if he killed himself."

"You think he'd kill himself?"

"Probably," Kim said. "So I have to figure something else out. You know there was this serial killer. I forgot her name. But she would go around in the children's ward and shoot the kids up with Succinylcholine. It is a muscle paralyzer. No way to trace it."

Kim would later inform Gowen that if she could kill Steve and get away with it that she "would do it tomorrow."

Seeking other alternatives aside from poisoning, Kim approached fellow surgical tech Ken Burges in the locker room of the hospital.

"Hi, Ken."

"Hey there," Ken said.

"Do you know of anyone that could kill my husband?"

"What?" Ken asked. He thought Kim was playing a joke.

"Do you know anyone that can, you know, kill someone? For a price."

"I'm insulted that you would ask me that. Do I look that sketchy to you?"

Burges had been convicted of welfare fraud in Virginia a couple of years before obtaining his job at the hospital. Because of this, Kim may have presumed that he would be the type of person who would know people capable of such an act.

"I got $50,000 for anyone who could do something like that."

"You got the wrong dude," Ken said. "The wrong guy."

"Forget I even asked," Kim said.

"You work in the operating room," Ken advised. "You could just put him to sleep."

Ken didn't know that Kim already had that idea in mind.

Kim began to plot out details of the murder. She needed to do something that was untraceable. This called for poison. She had to burn away any evidence so her attack had to take place away from home.

She ran her plan by a college friend of hers, Rachel McCoy. Kim justified her actions by demonizing her husband. She talked about his unwillingness to do stuff with her as he was a homebody and kept a messy home. Their personalities were too different.

Then without warning, she began articulating her plan to kill Steve with the poison and then setting the place on fire.

It was almost as if she wanted Rachel to poke any holes in her plan should she miss anything.

Rachel tried to talk Kim out of the hare-brained idea to no avail. She suggested simply getting a divorce but Kim was convinced that killing Steve was "easier." Rachel also brought up the fact that she was robbing their daughter, Anna, of a father.

"She would be better off without him," Kim said.

Whatever Rachel suggested, Kim had an answer for.

Her mind was made up.

Steve had to go.

CHAPTER FOUR

Kim knew that the drug she had to obtain was Succinylcholine. It would be readily available to her as she did her rounds through the hospital. Just walk by a tray of meds in the surgery unit and lift one of the vials. Easy peasy.

"I'm going to get this drug," Kim told her friend Rachel. "It will paralyze Steve. Stop his breathing and then I'll set the curtains on fire with a candle or a cigar. He won't be able to move and then he'll die of smoke inhalation. Nobody will know shit."

Kim would not take into account the fact that her husband was a healthy and robust man with no medical history. That would certainly draw suspicion.

"This would be the only logical explanation for what brought about Steven Hricko's death," prosecuting attorney Robert Dean said.

"Because there was nothing else wrong with him. His body organs were in fine shape, there was no trauma. It had to have been this. She had to have carried through her plan."

"Kim was determined," Orange said. "She wanted her cake and eat it too. It is a head scratcher as to why she didn't pursue a divorce but the mind of a sociopath works differently. She wanted a clean break. If she had gotten a divorce, then Steve would have remained in her life forever the next ten years because of their daughter. She wanted to erase him from the picture and nothing and nobody was going to talk her out of it."

The planned romantic getaway loomed on the horizon for Valentine's Day weekend. Steve looked forward to their alone time together with giddy excitement. He told his counselor that this would be the turning point where the sparks of romance would once again be rekindled.

But Kim looked toward the weekend with dread. She had told Jennifer Gowen that she had only had sex with Steve once in the past six months and the experience left her feeling repulsed.

"I'm not looking forward to the trip," Kim said in her own counseling session.

"Why?" her counselor asked. "It may be an opportunity to rekindle some passion."

"I'm tired and really don't feel up to the trip. It's a long drive. It is going to be miserable."

Then a light bulb flashed in Kim's mind. The resort would be the perfect place.

The perfect place to put her plans into effect.

CHAPTER SIX

Valentine's Day weekend arrived.

Steve had romance on his mind. His forehead perspired as he felt the anxiety of trying to save his marriage.

Kim had Brad Winkler on her mind as she looked out the car window.

Then her mind drifted to murder.

She had to set everything up just right. Inject Steve. Burn the cottage room. Then tell the police her story and stick with it no matter what.

Kim and Steve drove from their home in Laurel, Maryland to St Michaels. It would be a 75-mile to a romantic getaway that many had christened as the "Heart & Soul of Chesapeake Bay."

But the couple arrived at their cottage and found the place to be freezing. Kim started a fire in the wood stove then made some coffee.

The conversation was muted and awkward. They decided to watch some TV before looking out the window and taking in the view of the bay. It was windy and the the cold, damp weather chased them back inside

Preparing for the dinner, Steve popped a few Effexor tablets for his depression which had gotten worse in recent weeks. He also took an anti-anxiety medication called Xanax and a muscle relaxant called Flexeril.

Getting dressed, they attended the interactive murder mystery dinner called THE BRIDE WHO CRIED. The actors staged a re-enactment of a woman killing her soon to be husband. The actors encouraged audience members to ask the actors questions in an attempt to find out who the murderer was.

Kim enjoyed the play immensely. When the actors called for audience participation, she was one of two women who went out onto the stage and began asking questions like a detective.

The play now over, Kim and Steve returned to their cottage. Not yet having their fill of entertainment, the couple would watch the comedy film "Tommy Boy". They got a good laugh out of it but according to Kim they "still did not talk about our problems."

Steve then fell asleep.

Kim stood over him like a predator then went to the bathroom to prepare her lethal cocktail of succinylcholine. Building up her nerve, she finally did the move that she had been practicing in her head for two years.

Kim pulled aside the bed sheet and injected the syringe into his neck.

I'll burn the body. That will get rid of the puncture wound.

Kim also knew that the drug she administered only caused paralysis. It didn't affect a patient's level of consciousness.

So when Kim set the room on fire, Steve would know that he was being burned to death.

And he wouldn't be able to do anything about it.

The thought made Kim smile. She didn't want to just kill him. She wanted to make him suffer. To humiliate him.

Kim pulled the now paralyzed but awake Steve off the bed and dropped him to the floor. She doused his body with lighter fluid.

Kim, what are you doing? Steve looked up at his wife, unable to move or speak.

"Call it the perfect crime," she whispered in his ear as if reading his thoughts.

He stared straight up at the ceiling, catching Kim's movements in the corner of his eye.

He heard a matchstick strike against a box.

Then he felt a sharp pain race up his body as she set him ablaze.

I can't move, Steven thought as terror and pain engulfed him.

I can't breathe.

I can't breathe.

Kim, what are you doing?

I brought you here to save our marriage. I have done what I could do making this better.

I love you. Please don't do this!

Kim poured more of the lighter fluid onto Steve's body. She lit another match and threw it on him.

"She injected him with succinylcholine and watched him suffocate," Maureen said. "And lit him on fire. How much colder could it get."

CHAPTER FIVE

Kim Hricko walked into the resort reception area with a calm demeanor. She had her ear to her cell phone which was turned upside down.

"I need to talk to someone who works here," she informed desk clerk Elaine Phillips.

"I work here," Elaine said, expecting Kim's response being anything from wanting more towels to complaining about faulty air conditioning.

"My room is on fire."

"Is there anyone else in the room?" Phillips asked.

"Yeah," she said without emotion. "My husband."

"What room are you in?" Elaine asked, making her way around the corner of the desk.

Elaine and another hotel employee hurried into the courtyard of the resort.

"You smell that?" Elaine asked. "Something is definitely burning."

The two sprinted to cottage number 506 at the end of the resort. The door was shut but there was a tiny opening in the sliding door in the rear.

Smoke filled the room. They could barely see one foot in front of them. Kneeling down, one of the employees saw the the prone figure of a man inside. He crawled in, braving the smoke and pulled the body to safety on the back porch.

It was too late.

Steve Hricko, burned to a crisp.

The man had died with a Playboy magazine at his side with his pajama pants down at his knees as if he collapsed while masturbating.

"I want to see his dead body," Kim said as she milled around with the hotel guests watching the scene.

"I thought it was odd," one of the guests said. "Because no one had pronounced anyone to be dead yet."

Kim gave her statement to the Sheriff then called their best friends, Mike and Maureen Miller.

"It's the last thing you expect when you receive a phone call at night," Maureen said. "When the phone rings at night you know that it's not anything good."

"My wife answered the phone," Mike Miller said. "And sort of roused me a little bit and said that there's was an incident in Steve and Kim's room. Kim's requesting that you come down there as soon as possible.

The Millers were shocked at the sudden death of Steve. They were even more shocked at the demeanor of Kim when they went to console her.

"I didn't expect her to be anything less than a hysterical woman whose husband passed away," Maureen said. "She was the exact opposite. Just exact opposite."

Kim told everyone that Steve was drunk and made advances toward her. He groped and fondled her but she didn't want to have sex. They argued and she left the cottage.

Mike knew that something was fishy. His friend Steve was not a drinker.

Did Kim plan this out?

"They said the fire started because of him carelessly smoking," Mike said. "Steve doesn't smoke. All the years I've known Steve, I've never seen him smoke a cigarette, a cigar. He despised being around people that smoked."

An autopsy was performed and forensic pathologist Janis Amatuzio, like Mike Miller, quickly realized that something was amiss.

"Steven's body was found in a fire," Amatuzio said. "The major question for the forensic pathologist is that did he die of the fire or not. When there was no soot in the airways, when there was no damage to the lungs. It suggested that Steven was dead before the fire started."

"Steven was not drunk that night," prosecuting attorney Robert Dean said. "The drug tests and the autopsy shows that. Steve was not drunk."

The picture didn't fit. Steve was not a drinker nor was he a smoker. But friends and family could not believe the worst about Kim Hricko. The fun and outgoing mother could not have killed her own husband, the man who adored her for the past nine years.

Could she?

"Was she really capable of doing this?" Maureen asked. "Everybody was saying it but again, I ignored it and just pushed it back and said that she wasn't capable of doing it. Man, was I wrong."

CHAPTER SIX

Police began their investigation and discovered that Kim left a trail of incriminating conversations as well as evidence.

"Kim was too smart for her own good," Orange said. "She did her research on succinylcholine, did her research on the how quickly a body burns. But she did not know how to stage a killing."

Kim had left empty beer bottles in the room and a pack of cigars. The cigars would be the clue that blew Kim's story up in smoke.

Steve was not a smoker and the cigars she had left behind as evidence were not the kind to start a fire.

"There was an investigation as to how a fire like this could have started," prosecuting attorney Robert Dean said. "That fire could not have started by the ashes of a cigar."

Kim would state that after she and Steve had gotten into a fight she went for a drive. She wanted to visit Mike and Maureen Miller who only lived minutes away. She stated she had become lost. The prosecution thought that her excuse seemed odd as she had visited the Millers on numerous occasions. She also had a brother who lived only a few blocks away from the Miller home. And why had she not simply called them on her cell phone?

"I didn't want to wake anyone," Kim said when asked why she didn't call.

Her answer was incongruent as why would she worry about waking someone up with a cell phone call when she didn't have a problem arriving on their doorstep in the middle of the night?

Nine days after the murder, police would arrive at the home of a Hricko friend where Kim had been staying. They had a search warrant for her car but Kim felt the noose tightening around her neck. She ran to the bathroom room and locked it behind herself as the police entered the home.

Kim then swallowed a whole bottle of Xanax.

"Come out of there, Kim," the police yelled.

They busted the door down and saw Kim there in the bathtub, holding a razor blade over her wrist.

"I'll kill myself!" she screamed. "I'll fucking do it!"

The officers quickly subdued Kim without further incident. They then transported her to a psychiatric facility where she was put on suicide watch.

The trial would only last six days as the prosecuting attorney detailed how Kim staged the murder.

"She stated that he was sloppy drunk," prosecuting attorney Robert Dean said. "And that he wanted to have sex. She said they got into an argument and that she left for a few hours. She said she drove around and got lost. And then she returned to the cottage and saw that it was full of smoke and then she reported that the room was on fire."

The case against Kim was made by several friends, co-workers, and neighbors. They all testified about the affair, the plot to kill Steve and her desire to acquire the drug succinylcholine.

Kim Hricko would be found guilty of murder and arson. She would be sentenced to life in prison.

"It's sad that he (Steve) is not the one in the world anymore and she is," Maureen said.

"He was my best friend," Mike said. "And the fact that he isn't here anymore is pretty hard for me to take."

The other victim aside from Steve was their nine-year-old daughter. She lost both her father and her mother.

"Her child is the victim," Maureen said. "And is forever going to wonder which side of the family is telling the truth. Is it true that her mother was unjustly accused or is it true that she's a cold, manipulating, calculating murderer."

END

LOUISA MERRIFIED : POISON KILLER

ANA BENSON

Louisa Merrifield Biography

There is an ongoing myth that if a woman wants to murder someone, she will use poison. These claims are partially true because 40% of killers who used poison are female. Surely, women do have more opportunities to administer the dangerous concoction to their victims because they are the caregivers. The women cook food, take care of a household, etc. And in the past, poison was simply laying around in forms of different cleaning agents and rodenticides.

The poisoners would often benefit from their victim's death, and this happened in the case of Louisa Merrifield, also known as the Blackpool Poisoner. She wanted to inherit a nice property in a wealthy part of the town, and Sarah Ricketts was in her way.

Early life

Louisa May was born in 1909 in Wigan, United Kingdom. Her father was a Methodist minister while her mother stayed at home in order to take care of the family. Louisa May grew up in a very religious environment, and her father was quite strict. She didn't have the freedom to do what she wanted which resulted in Louisa's unhappy adolescence. The same feeling stayed with her throughout her life. Louisa May didn't finish school so she didn't get the proper education which could have improved her status. After all, her father didn't allow it because it was uncommon for girls to attend colleges back in the day. Louisa May was supposed to be just like her mother and manage the household.

Louisa was very unlucky in terms of the relationships as well. She wasn't an attractive woman. As a matter of fact, Louisa was short and stocky, so there weren't a lot of suitors coming her way. But she did marry a man called Joseph who was an ironworker. Joseph was a heavy drinker who would spend the majority of his days either at work or in a local pub. The couple had four children together. The marriage lasted until Joseph's death from liver failure. His body simply couldn't take the amount of alcohol he drank regularly. Louisa hated being married to

Joseph, and she eventually admitted to her friends that she felt relieved when he died.

It took Louisa only three months to find a new husband. The recent widow chose her lodger who was seventy-eight years old. Louisa was in her thirties, but she clearly wasn't bothered by this age difference. The lodger's name was Richard Watson, and the two were married for only two months. Richard suffered a fatal heart attack, making Louisa a widow for the second time. Having in mind the events that would occur later, some investigators did take a closer look at Richard's death but found nothing suspicious about it. The man was almost eighty years old, and it is very likely that he died from natural causes.

Louisa May wasn't a wealthy woman, but she longed for the money and the easy life. She often struggled to put the food on the table and wanted to provide the necessities to all of her four children. Since she couldn't find a way to earn more money from her work, Louisa decided to commit a ration book fraud. The entire country was in the war, and the supplies were sparse. Ration books were used in order to even the field and provide every family with just enough food, clothes, and other useful goods. But Louisa wasn't happy with the amount her family was getting. So she managed to put her hands on a total of seven ration books, giving her more than enough supplies. However, her crime was soon discovered which lead to a quick arrest.

The war was coming to an end, and the United Kingdom started dealing with the criminals who abused the post-conflict situation in the country. Louisa May was sentenced to 84 days in prison and she was locked up in 1946. That wasn't the end of her ordeal because as soon as she was released, three of her children were taken away from her. The government decided that she was an unfit mother and that the children should be placed in the institutions because they will give them all the care they needed. Left on her own, Louisa May felt lost. With two failed marriages behind her, she started thinking about tying the knot once again.

Marriage to Alfred Merrifield

Louisa May was forty-six years old when she decided to marry Alfred Merrifield. He lived in Blackpool and was a pensioner. Alfred was significantly older than Louisa and he was in his sixties. The man was in good health, except for the fact that he was slightly deaf. It is suspected that Louisa selected Alfred because she thought that there is no way someone her age would be interested in her. As previously mentioned, she considered herself to be below average when it comes to physical appearance, and the years haven't been kind to her either. She was a bit overweight and starting to lose her sight. Louisa had to wear thick eyeglasses in order to function properly.

Alfred was a mild-mannered man who liked Louisa a lot. She would later tell her friends that Alfred pursued her for months until she finally agreed to become his wife. It was clear that Alfred's money wasn't the motivation because his overall income was very low. The newlyweds struggled a lot from the very beginning of their marriage. The financial problems weren't something uncommon for Louisa, so she did her best to find more work. Alfred tried to help her out a bit, but no one would offer him any temporary work position.

The only thing Louisa did well was housekeeping. After all, she did take care of her family for years. She applied for various cooking jobs, as well as for nursing positions, but she would often get fired. Her past employers described her as a difficult woman who would often argue with her supervisors. Louisa also drank a lot, which was a habit she picked up from her first husband. Alfred and Louisa simply couldn't make things work when it came to the finances. His pension was too low, and she kept losing the jobs. In the end, they started selling or pawning their possessions in hopes they would be able to survive a month. It was a difficult life filled with ups and downs. They needed a break as soon as possible because worrying if they will have enough money to buy food next week was tiring. Therefore, Louisa Merrifield grabbed the local newspapers in hopes of finding any type of work that would fit her experience and qualifications. She saw an interesting ad in Lancashire Evening Gazette, and things quickly moved forward.

Meeting Sarah Ricketts

Blackpool is a well-known vacation spot in the United Kingdom. Overall, the city is quite wealthy due to the tourists who frequent this place in the warmer months. Sarah Ricketts was a middle-class woman and a widow. She lived alone in a bungalow in Blackpool, which was located at 339 Devonshire Road. The house was in a part of the city called Norbreck which housed many prominent families that lived in the area. The woman had plenty of money and could afford to have a live-in housekeeper who would take care of both her and the household. Sarah was disabled, and she needed help as well as the company. Considering the location and the terms, Sarah Ricketts expected that many people would respond to her newspaper ad. She was looking for a housekeeper and a handyman who would live on her property.

But Sarah was infamous for her behavior, and the majority of candidates were not willing to deal with her. As previously stated, she had plenty of money in her bank account, but Sarah still acted like a middle-class woman. The widow was quite short and tiny, but she would intimidate anyone around her with her fiery temper. She was a difficult woman, and her dietary habits were particularly strange. As a matter of fact, she loved to eat jam, often straight out of the jar. Afterwards, she would have rum and stout. Having in mind that Sarah Ricketts was seventy-nine years old, her food preferences were very odd.

Sarah Ricketts needed reliable help around the house, and as she was reviewing the applications, Louisa Merrifield's immediately stood out. She was married to Alfred Merrifield so Sarah thought that he would be a great addition to the household as well. After all, he would be able to fix things around the bungalow. Sarah didn't know that Louisa Merrifield had a sketchy history. It was omitted from the application because Louisa's goal was to present herself in the best possible light. Sarah's rushed decision eventually had terrible consequences.

Louisa and Alfred Merrifield accepted Sarah's invitation to work for her, and the couple arrived at the bungalow on 12th March 1953. Things were looking great in the first couple of weeks, and Sarah was happy with her choice. Louisa was fairly young and able to take care of Sarah. Her cooking was great, and Sarah enjoyed the meals Louisa would prepare on a daily basis. Alfred was in charge of the gardening, and he cleared out the overgrown area, making the front yard beautiful once again. Sarah was ecstatic, and she started trusting her live-in housemates.

The entire neighborhood knew how happy Sarah was with her choice because she didn't hesitate to talk about them to her friends. She even gave Louisa her checkbook in order to pay the bills without thinking twice about the possibility that the woman might abuse this power, and steal her money. But the tensions started to rise very soon. Sarah began complaining that Louisa is not feeding her well. Apparently, Louisa's meals were starting to get sparse and Sarah was used to eating more food. She attacked Louisa that she was spending the food money on alcohol instead of buying quality ingredients for the kitchen.

The arguments were frequent, but this didn't stop Louisa and Alfred to approach Sarah's family doctor. Louisa was certain that Sarah liked her and appreciated the help she had provided so far. Apparently, the elderly lady wanted to write a new will, and she needed to get the doctor's permission that she is sane and clear-minded. The doctor was taken aback by this request, but having in mind that Sarah Ricketts lived alone and had two estranged daughters, he thought that she really liked her new housekeepers, and felt the need to leave them her bungalow, as well as the rest of the property. The bungalow was worth £3000, which is somewhere around $119,000 in today's currency.

The woman seemed coherent, and her solicitor was summoned to her bungalow as well. Sarah told him that Alfred and Louisa were good people who deeply cared about her wellbeing and that she wishes to leave them her property. She thought they do an excellent job around the house regardless of their tiny quarrels and that they deserve to inherit the property after her death. The solicitor wrote down the changes. Since he didn't sense any danger behind this request and the woman seemed completely sane, the doctor gave his approval, and a new will was made on 9th April 1953.

Sarah had a tendency to change her testament every now and then because she was often getting into fights with her two adult daughters. The woman thought they were after her money and would do her best to blackmail the two by denying them the property. As soon as Sarah Ricketts made a new will, Louisa started plotting how to kill the elderly woman. She traveled all the way to Manchester with her husband in order to get the things she needed and put her plan into motion. Alfred was very friendly to the clerk who worked at the store, and the man remembered him afterward. The two of them talked about health problems, including Alfred's deafness. The clerk didn't ask them where they were from, but the fact that they traveled for an hour to buy rat poison which is sold almost everywhere might have raised a flag right there on the spot.

The poison was a powerful concoction called Rodine, and it was used for eliminating rats from the households. The poison itself is quite strong due to the amount of white phosphorous it used to contain back in the days. Rodine is still sold today, but the formula had drastically changed. White phosphorous can be found in different military weapons, such as incendiary munition because it burns brightly and quickly. It can be quite damaging to humans, especially if one ingests it. As a matter of fact, 15mg of white phosphorous is enough to kill an adult. It is very toxic and can damage liver, heart, and kidneys. White phosphorous can be easily detected because the body might give a bit of a glow if someone managed to get this chemical into their system. The majority of people will notice a strong smell of garlic around white phosphorous as well. Rodine was a popular way of getting rid of rats, mostly due to its efficiency, so having it around the house wasn't an unusual thing.

The poisoning

Things really started to change during April because Louisa was quite unhappy with her job. She started complaining to everyone who would listen to her about how difficult Sarah Ricketts was. As a matter of fact, Louisa painted her as a very complicated person who would complain about the smallest things. Since the woman was partially paralyzed, she didn't move around too often. However, Louisa told her acquaintances that Sarah would simply ignore the fact that she cannot walk on her own and call them up in the middle of the night because she needed help getting out of the bed. Louisa was also annoyed because Sarah told her that her cooking was horrible, and she eventually started refusing to eat altogether.

Louisa was apparently disappointed in Sarah because she told the delivery man who brought her a supply of alcohol that the couple was spending too much money on themselves and that she would very likely fire them soon. Louisa claimed that wasn't true, and that Sarah was simply being mean to them even though they were doing their best to provide her with the best care possible. The following days were very confusing because Louisa mentioned to a couple of neighbors that Sarah died. It was evident that she was still alive and in the house. When confronted with making false claims, Louisa simply told her friends: *"She's not dead yet, but she soon will be."* Surely enough, her sinister predictions will come true more sooner than later.

It was 13th of April when Louisa Merrifield decided that it was time to remove Sarah Ricketts from the picture. She prepared Sarah favorite meal and added a couple of spoons of Rodine to the jam. The woman started feeling sick right away because the dosage was very strong. As a matter of fact, Sarah was in unbelievable pain minutes after her meal. Unable to figure out what was going on, Sarah thought that she might be having digestion problems. Louisa helped her get to the bathroom, but Sarah was not feeling any better. She cried while in there, and her screams could be heard throughout the bungalow. Four hours have gone by, and Sarah completely lost the power of speech, unable to scream or speak to anyone. Five hours later Sarah Ricketts passed away. She died on 14th April 1953.

Louisa contacted Doctor Wood in order to report that Sarah is not feeling well. She didn't specify what exactly was happening with the woman. Even though Sarah Ricketts was old, she was fairly healthy. The woman didn't suffer from any chronic diseases, and the only thing that was sometimes problematic was bronchitis. However, it wasn't that frequent, so Doctor Wood didn't visit Sarah's home often. Since there was no hurry, the doctor decided to postpone his visit to the Ricketts' residence. But surprisingly, Sarah died the following morning. Knowing her history, Doctor Wood was certain right away that something was wrong. Yes, the woman was in her eighties, but she was perfectly fine the last time he examined her.

His suspicions were supported by Doctor Yule, who did a check-up on Sarah only a couple of days prior to her death because the housekeepers were asking for an approval in order to modify the woman's will. He asked the Merrifields what happened, and Louisa admitted that Sarah started feeling ill one day before her death, but she decided to contact Doctor Wood instead. According to her, she thought that he might feel agitated due to the fact that he already examined Sarah Ricketts recently. Louisa didn't fail to mention that Sarah wished to be cremated as soon as possible after her death. Doctor Yule found this even more strange because he knew the woman, and she never expressed her willingness to be sent away like that.

The autopsy

The entire situation was getting stranger as the more information came his way. Doctor Yule decided not to cremate Sarah's body, but to analyze it thoroughly instead. The law back then was not to issue a death certificate if anything seemed suspicious. The symptoms which were described by Louisa were very odd, and he needed to confirm that the woman wasn't killed. Doctor Yule decided to send Sarah's body to a coroner who would do a full autopsy.

After testing the tissues for any trace of poison, the coroner discovered high levels of white phosphorous in her liver. When he opened up the body, the internal organs had a faint glow to them which was quite alarming. Not to forget the garlic odor that filled out the room. This confirmed that Sarah died of phosphorous poisoning. Doctor Yule's concerns were confirmed, and now he knew that Sarah Ricketts was poisoned. He immediately alerted the authorities who zeroed in on her caretakers because they were always in contact with the woman, and had numerous opportunities to poison Sarah. After all, they were cooking her the meals and preparing food on a daily basis.

The investigation

Louisa and Alfred Merrifield worked for Sarah Ricketts for just over a month, and the woman clearly didn't know them well. They were the prime suspects from the very beginning, so the police started monitoring their steps very carefully. There were so many details that indicated that something was very wrong with Sarah's death. For instance, Louisa didn't feel sad when the woman passed away. Unsurprisingly to the law enforcement, she was excited because the bungalow belonged to her. Louisa was happy so she would constantly brag to her friends. Having in mind the peculiar way Sarah Ricketts died, the reporters approached Louisa a couple of weeks later to ask for a statement. She mostly focused on how much she disliked her husband, and that he was very boring. Louisa even implicated that he might have had an affair with Sarah which was completely untrue.

The police were familiar with the poison which was used in this murder, so they decided to search the bungalow in order to confirm it was available to Louisa Merrifield. After combing through the financial statements, they have discovered that the couple traveled to Manchester a few days before the murder. The police located the shop in which Rodine was bought, and they talked to the clerk who remembered talking to Alfred on that day. But this was still pretty normal due to the fact that numerous people used Rodine every single day. But knowing that the couple bought a full can of this poison gave them an advantage. The investigators thought that there should be more Rodine left in the bungalow because there is no need to use a whole can in just a couple of weeks. The poison is very efficient, and the can should still be in the bungalow unless they were covering up their tracks and getting rid of the evidence.

After a thorough search of the premises, the police officers didn't find a can of Rodine which suggested that the couple has thrown it away in hopes of not being discovered. Louisa and Alfred were in serious trouble because they remained the only suspects, and the police decided to arrest them right away. All the evidence were against them, and the fact that the United Kingdom still had a death penalty indicated that they might be facing this punishment.

The arrests and trial

Both Louisa and Alfred were brought to the station soon after the search of the bungalow was complete. When presented with the evidence, the investigators saw a change in Louisa's behavior. They told her about numerous interviews that proved she had talked about the death of Sarah Ricketts even before the poison was administered. Louisa tried blaming her husband, but this plan didn't work out well either. During Alfred's interview, the investigators did think that the old man was forced to follow Louisa's lead. He was deaf, and couldn't remember some of the key details of the whole incident. While the majority of detectives might think that the man was trying to save himself from the death sentence, the investigators working on this case actually believed that Alfred had little knowledge of the crime before it occurred.

Louisa and Alfred were brought to trial in July of 1953. Louisa defended herself by saying that Alfred cheated on her with Sarah Ricketts and that the two of them had a sexual relationship. Alfred once again had no knowledge of this, and the judge was certain that the man wasn't involved in the murder plot. Louisa continued to incriminate herself even further by refusing to admit that she talked about Sarah's death days before it really happened. However, multiple witnesses have confirmed this, and it was improbable that more than one person misheard her. Not to forget Louisa's behavior after Sarah's death.

The trial lasted for a total of nine days, and Louisa stuck to her defense that Alfred was having an affair with Sarah. However, the judge dismissed these claims, saying that Louisa is 'a vulgar and stupid woman with a dirty mind.' Louisa was found guilty of a first-degree murder and was sentenced to a death penalty by hanging. The judge was unsure what to do with Alfred because it was obvious that the old man didn't participate in the planning or the execution of the murder. In the end, the judge decided to drop the charges against Alfred Merrifield.

The aftermath

The public all around the United Kingdom wanted to know more about the Blackpool Poisoner, which was the nickname given to Louisa by the press. Everyone eagerly waited to hear what Alfred had to say about the murder and his wife Louisa. Since he was named as a beneficiary in Sarah's will, Alfred moved into the bungalow because it now legally belonged to him. He agreed to give an interview to national newspapers in which he talked about his marriage to Louisa. He admitted that he was very afraid for his own life because she had taken out a total of seven insurance policies on him. He was certain that she would have poisoned him as well if she wasn't in prison. Not to forget that Alfred admitted that Louisa abused him during their marriage which resulted in his bad health.

Louisa Merrifield was held in Strangeways Prison in Manchester. The judge has sent an official letter to the most famous hangman in the United Kingdom, and his name was Albert Pierrepoint. Pierrepoint accepted to be Louisa's executioner. He was experienced and didn't hesitate to execute women. The death penalty took place on 18th of September 1953 which was six months after the murder. She was the last woman hanged at Strangeways Prison. Louisa was buried inside the prison walls. Alfred did visit her twice before her death.

Alfred Merrifield continued living in Sarah Ricketts' bungalow for years after the poisoning, but the court ordered him to move out eventually. He continued to struggle financially and even appeared in local sideshows a couple of times. Alfred was eighty years old when he died in 1962.

KILLER CHURCH LADY : THE TRUE STORY OF BLANCHE MOORE

KATIE STONE

"People couldn't believe that she did what she did. People became fascinated that how could someone who on the surface could be so nice, could be capable of such a heinous crime." - Paula Orange

Blanche Taylor Moore was born on February 17th, 1933 in North Carolina, the fifth of seven children. Her father was Parker Davis Kiser, a self-taught minister who had both a drinking and gambling problem. Her mother, Flonnie Honeycutt, held little sway in the goings on in the Kiser household. Flonnie would work in the local mills, bringing home $40 a week. She turned the money over to her husband who promptly turned around and spent the money on younger women. Kiser did various odd jobs to support the family, primarily working in a saw mill then later as an insurance salesman. His primary occupation, however, was the seduction of women that he came across in both bars and churches.

The Reverend Kiser was a strict father and didn't allow any of his children to participate in school activities or spend hanging out with friends.

Living a double life, P.D. Kiser's gambling debts increased to the point where he made the decision to sell young Blanche off as a prostitute to pay off his debts which he incurred during card games.

After one losing streak, Reverend Kiser took his adolescent daughter for a drive and pulled over to the side of the road.

"I'm going to pull up under that tree," Kiser said. "When I do, I want you to go fuck that man."

"P.D. Kiser was an alcoholic and self-righteous country minister," said psychologist Kelleher. "Despite efforts to abstain from alcohol he always relapsed. Blanche's childhood was utterly destroyed by her father and she lived in a childhood prison of despair."

Blanche, desperate to leave the abusive household, married James Taylor in May of 1952. Blanche was nineteen years old at the time,

Taylor was twenty-four. She would give birth to their first daughter, Vanessa, in 1953.

Blanche was the typical Southern diva, confident in her ability to seduce any man she wanted but found the pickings slim in her small North Carolina town. She was attractive by most accounts, having long black hair and eyes that "were so dark they looked black."

"Blanche's face was sculpted in the high bird-boned features of the very prettiest Appalachian women," one researcher said. "Long, lithe, with generous breasts and a sleek round bottom perched on slender, perfectly shaped legs."

"She flew her small burgh of Tarheel by grabbing the first man who asked her to marry him. Young Blanche was left with one overwhelming wish for the future-to leave her perverse, sermonizing father and begin a new life that was far away from his abuse."

Finances were tough and Blanche was forced to work as a cashier at the Kroger supermarket. She would toil on the job for six years before giving birth to their second child, Cindi, in 1953. Still, she became a popular fixture at the market as folks would line up at her register just to have a quick chat with the friendly Blanche. She would remain a mainstay at the supermarket for decades.

"She was always friendly to customers and her co-workers," a former Kroger employee said. "You would have never guessed her as being unhappy or mean to anyone. Just wasn't in her."

Her tenure at Kroger's looked to be mixed, however, as Blanche could be moody. But the management hierarchy gave her high marks in her job performance and labeled her as a "good leader" as she trained other grocery checkers.

Still, a dark side emerged.

"She could be vindictive," said one co-worker who asked not to be identified. "If you got on her bad side, watch out. She was two-faced. Two-faced and underhanded. There was one incident where a large bag of cash wound up missing. Management would have to explain why her store was the only store that didn't turn a profit."

BAD MARRIAGE

By 1959, things had soured at the homefront. Blanche and James had several loud fights in public. Blanche was dragged behind a car on one occasion and in another she was confronted about an affair with a customer at the Kroger supermarket.

Despite her peculiar manner, Blanche would be promoted to "head cashier" which was the equivalent of a store manager in today's corporate climate. This was one of the few top positions open to Kroger's women employees at that time. She would also sell Tupperware at home parties which she used as a cover to seduce different men that interested her.

Her husband James seemed powerless against the woman he married. He worked as a furniture restorer but jobs were few and far between for the former military veteran who had just returned from the Korean War. James was described as a "burly man" that was "quick to anger." He spent the majority of his time editing sermons taken from the Glen Hope Baptist church and sending them overseas for missionaries to spread the gospel. He also began drowning himself in alcohol which was much to Blanche's disappointment.

"Blanche had, in essence, married a carbon copy of her father," forensic psychologist Paula Orange said. "James was like her dad in that he was a compulsive gambler and was horrible with money. He would disappear on the weekend and come back flat broke."

Her own father wouldn't behave much better, leaving Blanche's mother in 1960 as he vowed to "find himself a younger woman."

Blanche then acted out on her own. She continued to use the supermarket as her own personal singles bar, having affairs with numerous customers and male supervisors.

James would find out about her affairs and would threaten to leave Blanche. The two would continue to have violent, explosive arguments but ultimately James would never follow through on his threats to leave.

A NEW MAN

By 1962, however, Blanche would have her sights set on a new assistant manager by the name of Raymond Reid.

Reid was already married with two young children and initially spurned the advances of the slightly older Blanche.

But what Blanche wanted, Blanche got. It took three years of flirting to finally get Raymond to lower his guard. Blanche seduced the married man but continued to sleep with other male companions she met through the store.

To further complicate her life, Blanche's father had taken ill shortly after she arrived to make some sort of attempt at reconciliation.

Blanche remained at his bedside and helped to try and nurse him back to health. The elder Kiser, however, was too far gone. He died due to "heart attack triggered by chronic emphysema."

Doctors completely overlooked the fact that Kiser had suffered from violent stomach cramps, diarrhea, vomiting, delirium and a blue skin pallor.

This all pointed to death by arsenic poisoning but they had no reason to suspect Blanche of anything.

Noting the ease with she got away with her father's death, Blanche set her sights on the other man who was an obstacle to her happiness.

Her husband, James Taylor would suffer a near-fatal heart attack. His brush with death forced him to "get right with God" and he attempted to reconcile with Blanche.

"James Taylor's life trajectory was strikingly similar to that of Blanche's father, Parker Davis," Orange said. "Like Davis, he would find religion later in life and put on the pretense of a changed man. Blanche saw through it all, she herself was used to men using religion as a prop much like her father. But she put up appearances for appearance sake."

Blanche would later describe James as becoming "the perfect husband and father" but her six-year affair with Raymond Reid continued.

Despite their marital infidelity, Blanche would try and persuade Reid to attend church with her.

"I have been quite religious all my life, or I was," Blanche recalled. "I was very active in the First Disciples until the fire. After that, I just lost my interest in religion."

With his wife deeply entrenched in an affair, James would come down with the "flu" in September of 1970. He started to lose his hair, had diarrhea, swollen glands, blood stool and blue skin pallor. All the signs of arsenic poisoning yet no one who examined him was any the wiser. He would be hospitalized at the end of the month and die a few dies after his admission, shortly after Blanche brought him some ice cream.

Blanche would then help take care of James' mother, Isla, up until her death on November 25th, 1970. Doctors signed off on Isla's death as something attributed to natural causes. Inexplicably, they ignored the blue skin pallor on the woman as well as the undigested arsenic that remained in the Blanche's mother-in-law's stomach.

So within two months, Blanche had eliminated both her husband James and her mother-in-law, Isla. She was able to obtain a small portion of their estate and used the money to buy a home in Burlington, North Carolina.

Despite proceeds from these deaths, her co-workers thought she may have been "tapping the till" at work as there was no way she could afford such a home on the meager inheritance.

COAST IS CLEAR

Raymond Reid would decide to go all in on his affair with Blanche. He left his wife and children in 1971, a full nine years after first meeting Blanche. He got himself a small apartment and filed for divorce from his wife, fully expecting Blanche to become his bride.

Blanche would stop by at Reid's new place, cook him breakfast and sexually entertain him. She said that Reid was "helpless" without her.

This caused a stir not only in their workplace but in the small town in which they both lived.

"Mom never expected to spend the rest of her life by herself. She had too much to offer," said Blanche's daughter Cynthia Chatman.

"Reid was a very good man. He was good to us," said Vanessa, Blanche's other daughter.

Blanche herself didn't feel that way. As a future district attorney said while investigating Blanche's story, she would soon deem the young Reid as someone who "wasn't good enough, she wanted to date someone better. She was very blunt about that."

Blanche had a foul mouth and often said things that were inappropriate. Once she told the friend of her son-in-law, "you know what you really need? You need a really good blow job. If I went down on you, it'd probably kill you. You probably couldn't handle it."

She wouldn't limit her romantic encounters with the male supervisors like Reid at the supermarket. She targeted anyone she found handsome as when a new delivery man entered the store, Blanche said, "Man, I'd like to see the dick on that guy."

SEXUAL HARASSMENT

The highly sexual Blanche would claim sexual harassment during her tenure at Kroger's. A top company official named Robert J. Hutton paid a visit to her store. Blanche would contend that he made advances and fondled female cashiers.

"He reached him up my dress, exposed himself and grabbed my buttocks," Blanche said as she recalled an encounter with Hutton. "He had his pants down and asked 'Are you ready for this?'"

Blanche then picked up Hutton's pants and underwear as she fled from the store. EmbaRrassed, Hutton had to borrow a meat cutter's smock before exiting the store.

Blanche didn't return to Kroger's after the incident. She filed a sexual harassment suit and began seeing psychiatrists. One of her doctors, Dr. Jesse N. McNeil said in an affidavit that Blanche suffered from "depression, anxiety, and a serious suicidal condition. She felt completely alienated and antagonistic toward men and has not been able to maintain any meaningful social contacts with members of the opposite sex.

Her defense attorney would later dismiss the affidavit as "hyperbole" to bolster the charges of the sexual harassment suit.

It would later be revealed that Blanche had a flirtatious relationship with Hutton before she filed suit. She was on the lookout for someone "better" than Reid and thought that Hutton may fit the bill. But the relationship soured and Hutton ultimately lost his job.

Kroger would settle out of court with Blanche, paying the flirtatious young cashier a lump-sum payment of $275,000.

YET ANOTHER RUSE

Always on the look out for "quick cash," Blanche concocted a scheme to collect some fire insurance in 1985. A mysterious fire broke out at her home and Blanche put the blame on a local "pervert", a man that she claimed to have seen lurking around her property.

"I saw a man," Blanche said. "He was creeping around the side wall."

"Did you call the cops?"

"No," Blanche said. "He was, you know, touching himself. Touching himself down there. I screamed and he ran away."

Firefighters agreed that arson was the cause and did not question her tale of the unknown "pervert" who set her home ablaze. Blanche would take the proceeds from the fire insurance and purchase a mobile home.

A month later, however, the mobile home was burned to the ground. Blanche once again blamed a "pervert" whom she said followed her to the trailer home. The authorities believed her and she collected another fire insurance check.

"Really not sure what Blanche was doing with all this money," Orange said. "She had to have over a quarter of a million dollars on hand from inheritances and sexual harassment suits. She soon realized that money could be gained quicker through settlements as opposed to hard work."

Still on the lookout for a "new man," Blanche met the acquaintance of the Reverend Dwight Moore on Easter Sunday of 1985.

Moore was the pastor of the Carolina United Church of Christ. Divorced with two grown children of his own, the fifty-one-year-old preacher immediately caught the eye of the forty-two-year-old Blanche.

She introduced herself at the end of his sermon and complimented him on his speaking ability. He soon began "counseling" her as her impending lawsuit with Kroger came to a head.

The two got to know each other and Blanche was judgmental toward the Reverend when she found out that his own marriage ended when he was discovered to have an affair with another woman in his church. But Moore was taken by the beauty and Southern charm of Blanche and would not be denied.

"Moore saw Blanche as the innocent victim," Orange said. "She could do no wrong in his eyes and this blinded him to a lot of things, mainly the fact that she had instigated the flirtation and was still involved with Reid. And oh yeah, she just killed her husband. But Blanche saw opportunity in the Reverend. The preacher man was divorced and the pastor of a relatively small church. So she probably saw authority in that. She liked men in the authority, whether it be a manager at Kroger's or a man giving a sermon in a small church."

It began platonic enough, at first, the two began meeting for lunch then dinner on a "friends" basis. Blanche did begin dropping hints that they shouldn't be surprised if she married a "preacher man" in the near future.

"The Reverend was putty in the hands of a seductress like Blanche," Orange said. "Blanche could quote scripture then talk explicitly about sex. She put up a false front of a churchgoing woman but had a carnal way about her. The Reverend took one look at her and thought to himself 'we got a live one here!'"

Moore was smitten and his phone calls to Blanche increased over time. He would leave notes on Blanche's front door step which were sometimes intercepted by Blanche's daughters.

The Reverend would invite Blanche out to "get some ice cream" and the two would soon arrive together as church gatherings.

"She was dating both both the Reverend Moore and Raymond Reid," Orange said. "Her daughters believed that her relationship with Reid had cooled off but nobody told Raymond. Moore seemed none the wiser that Blanche was still seeing Reid. So Blanche was playing both sides against the other. If things worked out with the Reverend she would dump Reid."

Reid would not go away easy. He had abandoned his own wife over twelve years earlier in the hopes of eventually marrying Blanche.

"She couldn't just break-up with Reid," Orange said. "She was in too deep. She got to know his family and friends. The expectation was that they were going to get married but for whatever reason in Blanche's mind, she held out. So, rather than string him along further she decided to eliminate him from the equation."

Reid came down with a case of the "shingles" in 1986 as he developed a skin condition that would point to arsenical peripheral neuritis.

By April, he would be hospitalized with the same symptoms as Blanche's previous victims. This would include diarrhea, projectile vomiting and a loss of sensation in both his hands and feet.

Again, physicians dropped the ball in assessing these classic warning signs of arsenic poisoning. The doctors ordered special tests for "heavy metals intoxication" as well as a urine test which showed six times the normal amount of arsenic in Reid's system.

The report never reached the desk of the doctor's and Reid would continue to suffer.

Blanche would play the role of the dutiful girlfriend but again her inappropriate comments would be put on display when on occasion Reid's son Steve left the room with an attractive young woman. When the young man returned, Blanche asked: "Well, did you fuck her?"

The young man looked on in shock then denied the accusation.

"Well, why not? Growing boy your age needs some pussy once in a while. What's the last time you had some good pussy?"

DEVOTED GIRLFRIEND

When she wasn't harassing Reid's young son, Blanche would be by the side of the sick man on a daily basis. She put on a false front to Reid and his nurses, quoting the Bible and giving the impression that she was a compassionate, Christian woman attending to the needs of her boyfriend.

"She made quite an impression on the nurses on duty," Orange said. "They would testify later that she was the epitome of the caring girlfriend. She showed the man compassion and caring and the all thought that he was very lucky to have Blanche Taylor Moore in his life."

Reid would be diagnosed with Guillain-Barre Syndrome, an auto-immune disorder with the symptoms being muscle weakness, nerve-tingling and progressive fatigue.

"Raymond would die and be revived again," Orange said. "His heart failed and he would be declared clinically dead, losing heartbeat and respiration but the medical staff was able to revive him."

Blanche, however, would be waiting to provide "care" after the staff saved her boyfriend's life. She would come with a cup of processed food and eagerly feed Reed after his latest return from the dead. She would make a show of giving Reid her homemade pudding and specially made "milkshakes".

"Her demeanor was so sweet and unassuming that the nurses wouldn't even think of questioning her," Orange said. "They would nurse Reid back to health, get some of that poison out of his system then Blanche would come into the room with her 'concoctions.' It was literally one step forward and ten steps back for the poor man."

Raymond would recuperate then relapse again into respiratory arrest.

"Think of the worst flu you've ever had then multiply it by ten," Orange said. "Then you're resuscitated again and again. He was on a roller coaster for his life. Absolutely horrific. All the while, Blanche would witness Reid's battles with death. She knew she was the cause of it, with her arsenic milkshakes and pudding, yet she would stand there aghast, praying to the God above that Reid be delivered from the illness."

Reid would regain consciousness but remain confused. He would then began to recuperate and get his senses back. He would feel optimistic about his chances then he would relapse again.

Physical and psychological torture on repeat play.

This would continue for three months. Blanche seized the opportunity to have Reid create a living will. She named herself as executor and beneficiary to one-third of Reid's estate. The other two-thirds would be divided between his sons.

"Blanche had a way about her," Orange said. "She could talk just about any man into doing anything for her. A great deal of her ability to have gotten away with the things she did was her own persona. By this time, she had killed her father, first husband, and her mother-in-law with the exact same methods. Yet no one ever suspected anything or put two and two together, not even those closest to her. Her persona was so ingratiating and unassuming that it would be unthinkable."

After the will was drawn out, Reid's health rapidly deteriorated. In October of 1986, he was brought into intensive care suffering from renal and respiratory failure. He would die three days later as his body began bloating so severely that his skin ripped apart.

According to her daughters, Blanche seemed torn up that Reid had passed away.

Doctor's blamed Guillain-Barre syndrome but wanted an autopsy to be certain. Blanche declined, manipulating Reid's sons into agreeing with her that no autopsy be performed.

"Blanche was like most serial killers," Orange said. "Narcissistic. She thought she was special. She thought she was smarter than everyone else and that she would never be caught."

This now opened the door to a relationship with the Reverend Moore.

"The coast was clear," Orange said.

The Reverend accompanied Blanche to Reid's funeral. She had acquired over $30,000 from Redis's estate in addition to pilfering his safe deposit box and the safe in his home. Reid's sons also gave Blanche over $45,000 from their father's life insurance in the belief that "he would have wanted it that way."

"Then the Reverend didn't waste any time," Orange said. "After an obligatory period of grieving, the Reverend pursued her with great fervor until she finally relented and the two had a wedding date set for August of 1987, less than ten months after Reid's death. Blanche now had a sizable nest egg but most likely lost it all through audacious spending and mismanagement. She had money acquired from the sexual harassment suit, her first husband, and now money gained through her manipulation of Reid's will. She got addicted to the scheming. The game playing and manipulation. It was all an adrenaline rush to her."

THE PERFECT WOMAN

To Moore's family and friends, Blanche seemed like the perfect woman for him. She put on a front of knowing the Bible backward and forwards, having the personality of a "church lady" to match.

"Behind the scenes," Orange said. "Both the Reverend and Blanche knew better. She was a hot number to be sure and everything that was repressed in the Reverend now came to fore. He would now have his cake and eat it too, the Southern man's dream of having a woman who is a lady in church but a tiger in bed."

Things were looking rosy until Blanche was diagnosed with breast cancer. She had one breast surgically removed in order to stop the spread. She went into recovery and the couple pushed the marriage ceremony back another year, to November 27th, 1988.

Things were still not meant to be, however, as three weeks before the wedding the Reverend Moore came down with a mysterious illness all his own. He suffered from vomiting and diarrhea so severe that he had to be hospitalized. Doctors would discover an "intestinal blockage" in the preacher and he was forced to undergo surgery.

Blanche and the Reverend were finally able to tie the knot in April of 1989.

The wedding was simple and witnessed by only two church members.

"She had on a real pretty dress," Doris Pender said, one of the witnesses. "They were beaming. It seemed like there was electricity there. It seemed like they were very much in love."The two lovebirds would go to Montclair, New Jersey for their honeymoon and also visit the Reverend Moore's first grandchild who had just been born.

The honeymoon would be short-lived as the Reverend Moore collapsed on a homeward bound trip five days later.

"There are two competing stories," Orange said. "One is that he ate a pastry then collapsed. The other is that he was spraying insect repellent on some flowers outside his home. Blanche came back with a chicken sandwich for him which promptly made the Reverend sick."

The symptoms eventually grew worse and the Reverend insisted on going to the hospital. He was admitted to the Alamance County Hospital on April 28th and his conditioned worsened after Blanche delivered some "homemade soup."

The doctors inexplicably sent him home but Moore's condition would worsen after he consumed another one of Blanche's meals. She would then drive him to North Carolina Memorial hospital which refused admittance without a written order from Alamance County.

The Reverend had now retained forty pounds of body fluid while Blanche got the necessary paperwork. She would then relay to the Reverend's family that he "was fine, we're just going to do some tests."

Moore's symptoms mirrored that of Guillain-Barre syndrome, the medical staff became suspicious because of the speed of which the symptoms appeared.

"This go around the medical staff tested him for arsenic poisoning," Orange said. "They found huge doses of the poison in his system and immediately suspected that Blanche had given it to him."

The Reverend fought back successfully against the poison. He was able to recuperate and was released from the hospital.

"Reverend Moore set a medical record," Orange said. "The physicians on duty noted that he had survived a dosage of arsenic higher than anyone on record. There was enough poison to kill a moose. Yet the Reverend survived. Amazing."

The police were summoned and became suspicious when they began investigating the number of people associated with Blanche that had died under similar circumstances.

"She didn't do anything," the Reverend Moore said when asked by the police if he believed that Blanche was to blame for his illness. "No way. Not my Blanche. I think I must have inhaled poison while I was spraying the garden for pests."

But the police saw a pussy-whipped man when they saw one. They proceeded to question Blanche who would deny bringing any food to Raymond Reid while he was hospitalized. The claim was contradicted by hospital staffers who were on hand to witness Blanche force Reid to drink one of her "homemade milkshakes."

Investigating further, authorities found out that Blanche had tried to get the Reverend's pension revised so that she would be the principal beneficiary. Blanche became worried that they would test the Reverend for arsenic poison. She had her husband's hair shaved bald but investigating officials were able to obtain samples from the Reverend's pubic region and tested that.

"Both Dwight (Reverend Moore) and Raymond felt depressed," Blanche said when asked why both of her lovers tested high for arsenic. "They were probably taking arsenic themselves."

Police would charge Blanche with assault and had the body of Reid exhumed on his body, consistent with those found on the body of her first husband, James Taylor.

The chief medical examiner would discover that Reid's illness was not only the cause of arsenic but that he continued to receive the poison while he was in the hospital.

The Reverend would refuse to believe that his wife would do such a thing. It took six weeks but the police finally convinced him otherwise after they exhumed the bodies of Raymond Reid and James Taylor.

"You're lucky," the detective informed him. "Damn lucky you're even alive."

The Reverend then confronted Blanche about the accusations he heard from the police. He informed her that their marriage was over. The decision was an emotionally devastating one for the Reverend as Blanche left his hospital bedside covered in crocodile tears.

MOTIVATION?

The townsfolk and those close to Blanche immediately wanted to know why. Why would such a sweet and unassuming woman commit such diabolical crimes. The district attorney, however, couldn't care less. He just knew that the crimes had taken place.

"We don't have to get into why," the DA said. "When you start looking for a rational motive, you generally start overthinking. I just know that this guy died and the state medical examiner said he had a fatal level of arsenic in him."

Blanche was arrested and charged with the murder of Raymond Reid which the DA felt would be easier to prove than the Reverend's poisoning.

During the trial, which opened in Winston-Salem on October 21st, 1990, Blanche continued to deny giving Reid any food. The state produced over fifty-three witnesses who contradicted her statement. Reid's ex-wife and sons also sued Baptist Hospital for malpractice.

During her trial, jurors would discover how Blanche would kill her victims with kindness. She would place the arsenic in the food she would bring for him until ultimately he died.

"Raymond Reid lay in Baptist Hospital flat on his back, bed sores on his back, completely unable to move, tears in his eyes on the days that this woman who was killing him doesn't come," lead prosecutor Janet Branch told the jury, tears streaming down her face.

"He's crying because his murderer isn't coming to see him! Can you imagine anything more pitiful in this whole world? And he loves her with all his heart. ... But she's running around on him, and she's sleeping with Dwight Moore, and she's going to that hospital."

"I never felt the need for vengeance," Moore said. "I have no desire to see her executed. I don't even object to her efforts to get off death row. I have no feelings against her living out her final days in the most humane way possible."

"The authorities began to realize that they had a serial killer on their hands," Orange said. "They wanted to exhume the bodies of everyone that knew Blanche Taylor Moore in their lives. There was a bit of a hysteria going on. Ultimately, I think the authorities decided not to pursue the matter beyond what they could prove in court. The countless one night stands by Blanche would have been impossible to track considering her tenure at Kroger's."

They would exhume five bodies. Traces of arsenic were found in the bodies of both her first husband and her father.

She was cleared of any wrongdoing in her father's death but many believed that the trauma she suffered at the hands of her father led to her becoming a serial killer.

"Her father was a womanizer," Orange said. "And he had abandoned the family had some point. I think that perhaps she mirrored his behavior in her own life and took it a step further, taking out revenge on her father with the many men she came into contact with."

"It certainly isn't uncommon for female serial killers to carry bad relationships with their father into their future relationships with men."

"She is killing her father over and over again."

"I have no doubts as to her guilt," the Reverend Moore said. "The worst lingering effect has been tremors in my hands and weakness in my legs along with peripheral neuropathy. My feet and legs are pretty much a constant reminder (of Blanche).

Blanche Taylor Moore remains on death row in North Carolina. She is the oldest inmate on death row in the state.

www.ingramcontent.com/pod-product-compliance
Lightning Source LLC
Chambersburg PA
CBHW051838130726

47987CB00002B/605